HOME SELLER 411 *The Smart Guide to Selling Your Home*®

Your destiny can change by hearing the right words. It is our goal that your desire to sell your home will be made easier and less stressful by your choice to utilize this guide.

You can gain the knowledge that you need to sell your home in a manner that serves your and your family's best interest if you have the desire to do so!

You may feel at this time that you are ill-equipped to sell your home.

However, after reading this guide and applying what you will learn— your home selling experience will be a more pleasant one!

This book is designed to create the right atmosphere for the successful sale of your home!

ISBN: 978-1-953994-06-6

Table of Contents

Preface

What is the difference between those who sell their home the "smart way" and those who don't?

As the **Broker/Owner** of Realty 1 Strategic Advisors, LLC I have seen hundreds of **home sellers** apply the information contained in this book.

E-mail from them later reveals results that range from incredible success to providing the information at just the right time.

But why so many successful results?

What separates those who follow advice in this book and on our websites:

www.the-best-atlanta-real-estate-advice.com

www.realty-1-strategic-advisors.com

TheWealthIncreaser.com

Most people who utilize the information in this book and the websites listed above are just ordinary people who have a strong desire to sell their home in a smarter way.

They have focused in on the content in this book to maximize their home selling experience.

Some people take in valuable data throughout their life but fail to apply it in an effective way. It is if they hear and see the wisdom in the words, but they seemingly let the powerful information in one ear and out the other.

They never stop to seriously process and comprehend the power and significance of the information that they have received!

We all know that there is no 100% effective path to success when selling a home. The future is uncertain.

But there are clear habits that those who "do not" process and apply information to their advantage have. They are usually:

*procrastinators

*make excuses

*blame others

*are not trustworthy

*are not reasonable

*are envious of others

*are liars and cheaters

*like to criticize

*have attitude of a quitter

*think they know it all

There is always a reason why people don't apply valuable information. It usually resides inside them, but most people won't look inside to find it.

The information in this book is intended to provide you timely and sound advice that can help you enhance your home selling efforts.

We could write the same material as other real estate books that are on the market and watch as consumers sell their homes with no real understanding and regard for their long-term success.

And then watch them as they possibly sell their next home improperly due to not being properly prepared to sell or selling at the wrong time.

Even some of the biggest and strongest real estate companies go for the quick listing and sale at the expense of the seller's future well-being.

As a home seller it is important that you are willing to work toward selling your home the right way or a smarter way.

Not everyone wants the financial freedom and "peace of mind" that comes with selling their home the smart way.

The key as a consumer is to decide if you want to do it the right way or you just want to sell your house and move on at all costs.

Do you want to be a **home seller** and do the things in life that you enjoy or do you want to be bogged down with your future housing or rental payment and other debt?

Even those who are in a strong financial position and properly positioned to sell their home the right way will find great benefit with this book.

As we all know in real estate, no system can guarantee your home selling at the price that you desire.

Our unique services were developed over the past 20 years. **Home Seller 411** is my best effort to share what I have learned, to help you sell your property in a smarter way.

The blueprint is there, no longer do you have to make the mistakes of past **home sellers.**

Having said that, you may do everything right while attempting to sell your home and still encounter financial difficulty after selling your home due to some unforeseen event.

However, you will greatly reduce the odds of that happening if you prepare to sell your home the smart way—right from the beginning.

If you **sell your home** the wrong way, it can often end up in disappointment for you years down the road. It is important that you minimize the possibility of disappointment <u>by addressing your concerns on the front end.</u>

It is important that you have the drive to **sell your home the right way.** Those who want to sell the smart way realize the value and know that it is a better choice than **selling their home** just because they can.

This guide will provide the seller who desires to sell their home in a more effective way, all the resources that they need to put them in the best financial position prior to, while, and after **selling their home.**

Does everyone want to sell their home the right way? Of course not!

But if you do, this guide is here for you. Anyone who chooses to sell their home the smart way is a serious home seller in my opinion.

What about those who refuse to get their financial house in order prior to selling their home? My advice is for them to seriously reconsider that decision when possible.

It is important to realize that if you desire to sell your home effectively—you must get properly prepared to do so in a proactive manner!

It is important that you don't sell your home with reckless disregard for your financial situation or future goals!

If home sellers are not willing to make **positive changes** in their life to get into a more favorable selling position, they are not serious about long-term success.

*This book is designed to provide the knowledge that is needed for long-term success for **home sellers** in any market!*

There are many different types of financial statements available that can help you get a better picture of where you stand financially.

In the **Introduction** you will be presented with new trends in the housing industry, credit concerns that you should have—even as a seller, and tax concerns that you must be aware of after the sale of your home.

HOME SELLER 411 *The Smart Guide to Selling Your Home* provides you the information that you need so that you can succeed in today's real estate market.

HOME SELLER 411 is a step-by-step guide that is designed to better serve your long-term interest if you are considering selling your home in a smarter way.

HOME SELLER 411 *The Smart Guide to Selling Your Home*

Your destiny can change by hearing the right words. It is our goal that your desire to sell your home will be made easier and less stressful by your choice to utilize this guide.

You can gain the knowledge that you need to sell your home in a manner that serves your and your family's best interest. You may feel at this time that you are ill-equipped to sell your home.

However, after reading this guide and applying what you will learn, your home selling experience will be a more pleasant one!

This book is designed to create the right atmosphere for the successful sale of your home!

9

Introduction

What is the difference between those who sell their home the "smart way" and those who don't? It is a question that you must ask if you desire to be a successful home seller!

As the **Broker/Owner** of Realty 1 Strategic Advisors, I have seen hundreds of **home sellers** apply the information contained in this book.

E-mail from them later reveals results that range from incredible success to providing the information at just the right time.

But why so many successful results?

What separates those who follow advice that can be found inside this book, from those who don't?

If you are not properly prepared to sell your home and you do so anyway, you would be at more risk to possibly receive less in sales proceeds from the sale of your home due to not being properly prepared to sell in a manner that worked for your best interest—and your future goals would be less likely to occur.

In the real estate industry, even some of the biggest and strongest real estate companies and home selling companies often go for the quick sale at the expense of the seller's future well-being.

Not everyone wants the financial freedom and "peace of mind" that comes with selling their home the smart way.

The key as a consumer is to decide if you want to do it the right way (smart way) or you just want to sell your home at all costs.

Do you want to be a **home seller** and do the things in life that you enjoy or do you want to be bogged down with your housing or rental payment and other debt?

Even if you are already in a strong financial position and properly positioned to sell your home the right way, you will still benefit from this book. As everyone knows in real estate, no system can guarantee you the selling of your home at the price that you may desire, as there are too many life and economic variables.

However, by purchasing this book you will obtain powerful home selling knowledge that I have discovered over the past 20 plus years. This book is my best effort to share what I have learned to help you sell your home the right or smart way.

The blueprint is there, no longer do you have to make the mistakes of past home sellers.

Having said that, you may do everything right while selling your home and still face difficulty due to market conditions or due to some unforeseen event!

However, you will greatly reduce the odds of that happening if you sell your home the smart way, right from the beginning.

If you sell your home the wrong way, it can often end up in disappointment for you years down the road.

The goal of this book is to help minimize the possibility of homeowner disappointment that you might encounter from the sale of your home by addressing your questions or concerns on the front end.

This book is written for those who have the drive to **sell their home** in a smarter way or in a way that is more favorable for them and their family in the current economy—or any economy.

Those who want to **sell their home the smart way** realizes the value of doing so and know that it is a better choice than **selling a home** just because they can.

This book will provide the seller who wants to get properly prepared to sell their home the resources that they need to put them in the best financial position prior to, while, and after **selling their home.**

Does everyone want to sell their home the smart way? Of course not!

But if you do, this book is here for you. Anyone who chooses to **sell their home the smart way** is a serious **home seller** in our opinion and will be in a better position to purchase their next home by gaining the needed knowledge on the front end.

There are many different types of financial statements available that can help you get a better picture of where you stand financially and put you in a better position for homeownership.

In the following paragraphs you will learn about new housing trends and how you can use personal financial statements, credit and tax awareness and a comprehensive approach to managing your finances to position yourself for a more prosperous home selling period.

By doing so you can achieve more during your lifetime and make the process of selling your home a more enjoyable experience.

New Trends in the Housing Industry

Over the last twenty years or so there have been many changes happening in the housing industry and in some cases the changes have been groundbreaking. Home buyers now have many options for purchase—and as a potential home seller, you too have many selling options.

You have the option of selling your home as:

1) A lease purchase—however, make sure your property is in optimal selling condition if you choose this option.
2) A land contract—seller keeps deed until final payment—buyer(s) can't leverage a land contract, generally speaking.
3) Traditional financing—using a bank, mortgage company, mortgage broker etcetera.
4) Creative and non-traditional borrowing (seller note, hard money lenders, owner financing etcetera).
5) Cash sale
6) Sell directly to a home buying company or brokerage company.

In the future you can look for home buying companies, real estate brokerages and other companies that offer to buy directly from the homeowner to increase in number, thus eliminating the need of a home seller to list their property with a real estate agent in the traditional manner. And with the recent COVID-19 and other public health concerns—many who once never considered a home purchase are now considering ownership options as opposed to renting.

Many millennials are now considering homeownership--and the effect of mortgage interest rates will play a large role in homeownership decisions—as well as builders and communities offering amenities that attract certain demographics—particularly to attract millennials. In many areas of the United States there is a shortage of affordable homes that make it feasible for those with modest income to even consider owning a home.

Many affordable homes will be farther away from the central city area and the use of new technology (artificial intelligence) will become more prevalent. Even though the entry level homes in some areas are priced out of the reach of many middle-income and working-class families, the luxury home market is expected to continue to increase in future years.

Homes are now being listed and sold on many technology platforms, auction sites, by investors and even on the courtyard steps when foreclosure occurs. And there are now many "home selling and home buying" companies competing with home buyers for purchase. Many are also competing directly against home sellers and many others are popping up at a dizzying pace.

Many new companies that are now in the marketplace often purchase all cash and resell to buyer's months later after doing cosmetic or in some cases major repairs or upgrades. Still others will buy and hold and rent out for years and cash in (sell) at a date far into the future.

What are home seller's doing to counter this new reality?

Home sellers are "now proactively taking action" to ensure that their finances are in order well before their home goes on the market— and a thorough analysis of their tax position and how the selling of their home intertwine with their future goals are now being analyzed in a more serious manner—proactively as opposed to after the fact (after home is sold).

In the remainder of this introduction, you will learn about these new home selling trends in greater detail so that you can properly prepare on the front end and furthermore get a better feel for who and what you might be competing against in your real estate market when you decide to sell your next home.

Even in a changing economic environment, selling your home in the current economy can be a wise choice if you are properly prepared and you have done your homework well in advance of receiving your offer to purchase from a potential buyer!

In the past decade and particularly since the COVID-19 era, the "home selling environment" has had many new entrants outside of traditional home sellers who sell their home using real estate companies or sell directly as the home seller.

Even so, is it a wise or good decision to compete among the new entrants into the real estate market as a home seller when it comes to selling your home?

In many areas, home selling companies from old entries (**we buy ugly houses—Homevestors** etcetera) to new entries (**Redfin**, **Zillow**, **Open Door**, **Real Estate Companies**, Ownerly, **iBuyers** and **Investors**—along with other players in the market) have been advertising in an aggressive manner to get potential home sellers to utilize their company in the selling of their home in a hassle-free and less burdensome manner.

Are these new approaches to selling your home a wise or beneficial approach for you to compete against?

Like most things in life—it depends.

However, <u>you want to ask and answer a number of questions upfront</u> prior to selling your home.

And with the increase in technology and home buying and selling platforms, new entrants into the market and uncertainty over home inventory in many parts of the United States and throughout the world, many are asking—what is the best approach to take for those who desire or need to sell in the current market?

Credit Concerns & Home Selling

There are a few concerns that you should address if you are considering selling your home at this time or in the near future, as by addressing those concerns it will help you whether you are in a buyer's market or a seller's market and whether you are selling or buying a new home or a resale home during difficult economic environments that may be present, or that will arise in the future.

Although addressing credit concerns prior to home selling is not a new trend over the past twenty years, gaining a comprehensive and highly effective mastery of credit prior to your home sale is a new trend as it will play a major role in ensuring that you remain a homeowner well after your home sale.

It is very important that you as a potential home seller understand your credit position prior to selling your home—as well as after.

You should proactively know your credit position as there are now many free or low-cost credit reporting and credit scoring companies on the market and there is no excuse for you not knowing at a minimum the likely range of your credit score and if you have derogatory information on your credit report that needs addressing prior to selling your home.

Keep in mind that most credit scores by many providers will not be the same as those used by mortgage lenders or mortgage brokers, however they will provide helpful guidance that will at a minimum "put you in the know" as far as what you would potentially pay interest rate wise if you had a desire to purchase another home after the sale your home and you wanted to us financing.

It is important that you know "the five credit factors" and how to apply them to your unique credit and financial situation so that you can efficiently reach the success that you desire, and particularly the home selling success that you desire or need to experience.

Even as a home seller it is important that you have a "workable understanding" of how to apply your knowledge of the **"5 credit factors"** that you need to know and will soon learn, to move yourself and your family forward in a timely manner throughout your lifetime—or at a minimum during the period of your life that you will utilize credit or plan to utilize credit.

There are two major credit scoring algorithms, and they are **FICO** and **Vantagescore** and you want to be aware of both.

Although the factors used by the two major credit scoring algorithms vary somewhat, by mastering the factors that either credit scoring system uses you will effectively manage your credit and credit score with both scoring models—and potentially reach your intended goals.

Did you know that your **credit score** shows your potential and current lenders if you have been responsible in your use of credit?

If you are now unaware of **"the 5 credit factors"** learning how to proactively utilize them prior to putting your home on the market is a great time to gain a comprehensive understanding of what they are!

However, it is also critical that you properly utilize that understanding throughout your life so that you can maintain or improve your **FICO (Fair Issac & Company) score** and **Vantagescore** so that you can achieve other goals that you may have, even after your home sale.

Fair Issac & COmpany (FICO) takes information in your credit file at each of the **3 credit bureaus** and puts that information into a mathematical formula (algorithm) to calculate your credit score.

Your credit score will fall in the 300 to 850 range with most scoring models and your goal should be 720 at a minimum if you have a need or plan on using credit in your future—and particularly before you sell your next home.

Potential lenders in the United States will use your **FICO score** to determine if you are a good credit risk for lending purposes and will use your **FICO score** to determine your interest rate using "automated underwriting" on particular types of loans (i.e., your credit card, auto loan, mortgage loan etcetera).

There are 3 major credit bureaus that compile credit scores:

Transunion

Equifax

Experian

You can always know the 3 credit bureaus by thinking that you are **TEE**ing off with your swing—however you are not golfing but improving your credit and credit score by **TEE**ing off on your credit!

You can get **all 3 credit reports for free** once per year from each credit bureau (**T**ransUnion, **E**quifax and **E**xperian) by going to:

www.annualcreditreport.com

The industry standard credit score can be found at **myFICO.com**, however each credit bureau have their own scoring system **(as well as a FICO score)** and many lenders will use the average or middle score of the 3 credit bureaus to determine if you are a good credit risk.

On the following pages you will learn an **empowering pathway that provides you the route to the mastery of your credit** and you will have the opportunity to implement a realistic path toward the credit success that you desire in a manner that allows you to give it your absolute best!

It is important that you comprehend and apply what you need to apply to improve your credit. By gaining a comprehensive understanding and application of the **five factors that affect your credit score** you will be in position to open a new door.

Be sure to utilize a comprehensive approach in the management of your credit and credit score so that you can attain more success for yourself and your family and achieve more success in all your credit endeavors throughout your lifetime.

It is imperative that you realize that what you do behind the scenes when no one is looking **(i.e., mastering the five credit factors)** is very important and prepares your mind with the "mental working knowledge" that is needed for you to achieve at your highest level of excellence when you come from behind the scenes.

You must be circumspect in the management of your credit and finances due to the time that we now live in. Or another way of looking at it is that **you must use due care** in the management of your credit and finances from this day forward if you are to achieve more during your lifetime!

It is important that you are <u>operating in your purpose</u> at this particular <u>TIME IN YOUR LIFE or you are taking action to do so at this time!</u>

The following "5 Credit Factors" will get you moving fast toward your credit, financial and life goals and prepare you for a more successful home ownership or rental environment before and after you sell your home!

<u>Negative Information or Payment History—35%</u>

It is "very important" that you keep "negative information" off your credit report, and you have a real knowledge of how your "payment history" **on** and **off** your "credit reports" affect your credit.

<u>Utilization or How You Use Your Credit—30%</u>

It is "very important" that you have a real knowledge of how your "utilization" or how you "use your credit" affects your credit and credit score.

<u>Time Length of Accounts—15%</u>

It is important that you have a real knowledge of how your "age of your accounts" affect your credit and credit score.

<u>Type of Credit—10%</u>

It is important that you have a real knowledge of the types of credit (your credit mix) that you have in your credit file as it can help or hinder your credit score.

Inquiries or Hard Pull by Creditors—10%

It is important that you have a real knowledge of why you must keep the "hard pull" of your credit file to a minimum if your goal is to build your credit.

You have just learned 100% of the credit factors (generally speaking) that are used by those in the credit industry to rank your credit score!

Don't feel you can remember the five credit factors? You can use this highly beneficial acronym as an aid to help you manage your credit effectively and efficiently throughout your lifetime.

Remember NUTTI, MUTTI or PUTTI **(you choose the word that works better for you—or choose all three)** *in your GUTTI to improve your credit score—forever more!*

N M or P in the above acronyms means:

N = Negative Information—you must keep negative information off your credit reports

M = Mess Up—you can't mess up your credit

P = Payment History—You must keep your payment history positive

U = Utilization

T = Time

T = Type

I = Inquiries

Review what you have just learned in your mind to "drive it home" and you should be able to know and manage the **"5 credit factors"** in a manner that will provide you the results that you desire throughout your lifetime!

Always keep in mind the **descending weight** of each credit factor:

N = 35%

U = 30%

T = 15%

T = 10%

I = 10%

Total = 100%

By mastering the 5 credit factors you will put yourself in position to **operate in excellence** when it comes to managing your credit and finances throughout your lifetime!

Also be aware that **you may see (or hear) other words** describing the **"5 Credit Factors!"**

However, it is your responsibility to line up what is being said (whether written or verbal) in the proper context "within your mind" because you have **"mastered the 5 credit factors"** at a very high level!

Also, be sure that you are aware of possible changes in the **FICO algorithms** and even the **credit factors** as there are always the chance that those in charge will make adjustments that differ from what you are now reading and learning.

Even what you have learned in the preceding paragraphs is not definitive but is the best of what is publicly available based on how those in the **credit scoring industry** operate.

That means that their way of scoring is unknown in some respects, however if you "master the 5 concepts in this discussion" you will have no problem achieving your credit goals.

In summary, **to effectively manage your credit and credit score** you mostly need a credit history with several accounts, no reported late payments, as well as low reported balances on your revolving debt (primarily your credit card debt).

However, by having a comprehensive understanding of the 5 credit factors you will be in a stronger position for long-term success!

NOTE: Also realize that **your credit score is one of many in a large pool (millions upon millions of other consumers who have a credit file)** and your score will fall in the lower, middle or upper range (300 to 850) and many <u>lenders will be more or less favorable toward you depending on where you fall in that range.</u>

In addition, if you have a joint account, authorized users on your account or you co-sign for a loan be aware that those who share your account can kick your score downward if they are irresponsible in their use.

*Another way of looking at it is if you share your credit with others in an "irresponsible way" they can **jack** up (or maybe **JACK "down"** is more appropriate) your credit score and make reaching your goals far more difficult than it should be.*

You must realize that "you" are ultimately responsible for the **"timely payment" on your account(s)** whether you alone use the credit or other individual(s) are on your account(s).

Once you get your credit to where you desire that it be, you can then relax some—but always remember (and do your absolute best) to keep your revolving balances low or non-existent and always pay on time!

It is important that **you know where to go to find credit resources** that will make your journey of credit management more concise and will get you to your destination faster! You can use your favorite search engine to find timely topics on credit that can keep you up to date on happenings in the credit industry.

A **properly funded emergency fund** along with a "mindset of personal responsibility" will help ensure that you are in position to pay your creditors in a timely manner and also help **protect you from unexpected events** that will occur during your lifetime!

Once your **credit score** is in the range that you desire it will be as if you are driving on the autobahn—with no traffic in front, on your side, to your left or to your right (you will have no need to be concerned about what is behind you).

You will be in cruise control **(as you should be based on the "commitment" that "you made" to master and seriously apply the "5 credit factors" in your life)** doing the speed—or more appropriately **"achieving the goals"** that you desire—almost effortlessly because **you have made it a priority to master the 5 credit factors** and you know how to use that mastery to your and your family's best advantage.

By "proactively getting out in front of your home sale" (prior to running into financial difficulty or correcting those difficulties prior to sale) at the earliest point possible in your "life stage" you can make the right choices and make better decisions so that when you get older and look back you can have a feeling of exuberance as opposed to regret.

It is important that you don't needlessly waste time, energy and money by not having the "mental working knowledge" that is needed to manage your credit and finances in more effective ways as that is an inefficient approach to pursuing your dream of selling your home at a price that is favorable to you!

The time and energy that you are spending reading and comprehending what you are learning in this introduction and book will provide you the nucleus to achieve at a higher level throughout your lifetime!

Don't get too high or too low about where you now are because you are not comfortable about the overall process of home selling as the process will be made clear to you once you complete reading this book!

You will soon have a "complete picture" of how you can effectively manage your credit and finances throughout your lifetime and sell your home from a more advantageous position.

By starting on a serious path to managing your credit comprehensively, you put yourself in better position to make all your dreams a more realistic possibility.

The **decision** by you at this time to "manage your credit comprehensively" can put you on a serious path to **mastering the 5**

credit factors that affect your credit scores and position you and your family for a lifetime of credit and financial success.

In this short book you will also learn how to use personal financial statements and learn ways to manage your finances in a more comprehensive manner—prior too, while and after your period of homeownership in which you have sold your primary residence!

Tax Concerns & Home Selling

New home selling trends over the past twenty years also include that sellers understand their tax position prior to home sale—as well as after their home sale.

You should be aware proactively of the potential tax advantages (or disadvantages) that you as a home seller have when selling your home.

Capital gains and the exclusion from taxes criteria is something that you would want to know about.

The principal residence exclusion is an Internal Revenue Service (IRS) rule that allows people who meet certain criteria to exclude up to $250,000 for single filers or up to $500,000 for married filing jointly in "capital gains tax" from the profit they make on the sale of their home.

As a current homeowner you should be aware of many of the tax advantages of a homebuyer that was detailed on the **Closing Disclosure** and on your **1098 statement** that you received during the tax season from your lender or loan servicer the following year after your home purchase—and annually thereafter.

On the **Closing Disclosure** (formerly the HUD-1) and on your **1098 statement** that you receive at income tax filing time, your buyer (and you if you plan to purchase in the future using financing) may be able to use the following to help reduce your tax exposure:

- Discount points
- Prepaid interest
- Prepaid private mortgage insurance (PMI) or MIP
- Reduction in taxable income if you are first-time homebuyers and you used funds from your IRA to purchase your home
- 1031 like-kind exchanges (can defer or avoid taxes on rental property or personal residence that you converted to a rental)
- Energy credits and exemptions that the IRS allows (ask your tax professional what is available as credits change on occasion)
- Property taxes paid at closing and annually thereafter
- Mortgage interest paid throughout the year

I'm sure you kept the **Closing Disclosure (or HUD-1)** and **1098 form** as part of your tax records and provided it to your CPA or tax professional at tax filing time over your years of home ownership.

I'm also sure you took steps to ensure that you wouldn't lose your closing disclosure documents and other important paperwork during the process of moving into your current home.

As a current homeowner, you understand some of those closing costs on your closing documents are tax deductible and could ultimately lead to more money in your pocket.

If you purchase another home (using financing) after selling your current home, you will also receive a form **1098 mortgage statement** from your mortgage lender prior to your tax filing in "the year after purchase" that can also possibly help reduce your taxes and you would want to provide this information to your CPA or tax professional, as that too can lead to more money in your pocket (you'll pay less in taxes or get a larger refund).

Also, be sure to file for your **homestead and other exemptions** at the earliest time possible in your state or locality as that can lead to you paying less on your property taxes on an annual basis.

In the following paragraphs you will **learn key factors** that you must be aware of if you are to make your home sale and future ownership period more enjoyable.

- **Sell your home with the end in mind**

When you initially purchase your home, you want to have an idea of what you plan to do at the end of your home ownership.

Do you plan to purchase the home that you are considering <u>with that approach</u> in mind?

It is important that you ask the following questions prior to your home purchase?

Do I plan on selling, transferring to my heirs, renting for income, refinancing for cash or income, <u>selling for a gain</u>, doing a like-kind 1031 exchange or remaining in the home until I transition?

It is in your best interest to make a determination at the time that you purchase your home generally speaking—not years down the road <u>when you possibly</u> have to make a bad choice!

Having said all of that, <u>adversity or unwanted occurrences in life</u> can throw even the<u> best of planning</u> into a spiraling nightmare where you are<u> forced to make moves</u> that you would rather not make. Furthermore, you may not have been aware of your need to purchase your home with the end in mind—prior to your home purchase if you are now reading this book and you already own a home!

And with home prices and interest rates rising and falling in many areas, deciding whether and when to purchase can at times be a difficult choice. Even if you have a home to sell, you still need a place to stay, and it is important that you make the best decision that you can—as housing costs are on the increase, not decrease in most areas in the United States and are also rising in many parts of the world.

Even so (on your next home purchase), it is in your best interest to purchase your home with the end in mind so that you at least have some control over where you can possibly go in your future—and thereby reduce the likelihood of being pulled in directions that are not of your choosing.

- **Determine on your own what the home that you desire to put on the market is worth**

Most companies that offer to assist you in selling a home use computer generated estimates using factors in your area or zip code, such as sales data, taxes, trending data etcetera and CMAs (**C**omparative **M**arket **A**nalysis) to help you determine an offer price.

If you were to "list your home" with a real estate company, you would sign a "listing agreement" so that they can offer you the best service possible and help eliminate concern over losing the commission.

Be sure you are aware of "wholesalers—once frowned upon by the real estate industry, they are now normalized and can be found in abundance. They act as a middleman in transaction (seller—

wholesaler—buyer) and their goal is to offer a contract to sellers for less than market value, get seller to agree and then assign the contract to another buyer for a higher amount than they offered you.

In this scenario you could lose substantial equity that you had built up in your property, and in almost all cases you want to avoid using wholesalers to sell your property.

Many new home selling (and home buying) companies that are on the market make offers to sellers and use computer generated estimates using factors in your area or zip code, such as sales data, taxes, trending data etcetera, to make offers on homes and later resell to buyers at an adjusted price after cosmetic or major repairs have been made.

They are called iBuyers and they have entered the markets of many communities over the last 10 years. They often use a platform technology that is algorithm-based, with the goal of making market-based offers to sellers for their homes, and then selling those homes to buyers for a profit. These algorithms are commonly referred to as AVMs or Automated Valuation Models.

In other cases, some real estate or home selling/buying companies will list a seller's home and guarantee to buy at 80% or some other figure based on listing price if the property does not sell in a certain time frame.

Still others will offer to get buyers into a home of their dream and purchase their current home that they own (and are trying to sell) immediately or later, for a negotiated price.

As a seller in the current market, you may be competing against companies that will offer to purchase a seller's home as-is (and for all CASH) and will even offer to allow the seller to stay there 30, 60, and even up to 90 days after closing—making it hard for you as a home seller whose buyer(s) may require financing in the traditional manner, to compete against!

Many of the new home buying and selling companies will even make an offer on a home without having seen the interior or having an inspection of the property as a contingency.

As an informed seller and future home purchaser, it is important that you never make an offer on a home that you have not seen the interior and/or exterior of or one that has not been properly inspected unless you are prepared for the consequences as there could be major structural and non-structural concerns that will be your responsibility after you close.

You want to know the needed repairs and or upgrades upfront and have the seller correct them prior to closing—or if done after closing you at a minimum will know what needs to be done to bring your property up to the standards that you desire and possibly the cost range of the needed work.

Always keep in mind the fact that you will have to pay to live somewhere—and keep that at the <u>forefront of your thought process</u> as living expenses (including housing and rentals) are on the rise in most areas. Be particularly cautious of "new home sales" as you want to have proper representation and purchase on a good lot and in a good neighborhood and do inspections along the way.

You also don't want to overpay, and you want to utilize a quality builder and preferably buy in an area with strong school systems. By selecting an agent that will truly work in your best interests, you can ease the process of buying your future home, considerably.

- **Choose the best option based on your unique circumstances**

Are you now forced to sell your home or is time on your side? After you sell are you purchasing your next home as a short sale or distressed sale? Do you have pre-approval from your lender so that you can present a more competitive offer if you will be purchasing your future home in the traditional manner?

These and other pressing questions will help in your decision-making process as to how to sell your home and structure the closing time frame!

Do you have an <u>emergency fund</u> that is properly funded?

Do you have <u>little to no debt</u> outside of your anticipated mortgage payment and <u>do you have all areas</u> of your finances addressed at this time?

Do you have the <u>needed cash flow on a monthly basis</u> that allows you to live at the level of comfort that you desire? Have you reached your <u>retirement number</u> (or are you on a realistic path to reach that number) or is that number a mystery to you at this time?

If you answered in the affirmative to any (or preferably all) of the above questions, you may be in great position to sell your home and do the needed upkeep/repairs and live out your dream of selling your home and moving into a new home or rental.

In many areas of the United States resale homes are in short supply and that could work in your favor, depending on your future goals and your local real estate market!

If you are forced to sell in a non-traditional manner, at least get your debt to a manageable level prior to closing—not after if possible!

If you are in position to properly sell your property and you decide to use a real estate agent, be sure to use a real estate agent who works the area of your intended sale and has a track record of success.

Be sure to choose a reputable company and agent and get comparable home data based on realistic comparable sales data—and not just listings in the area.

You must negotiate effectively when selling your home!

It is important that you realize that there are buyer's and seller's markets that occur on an ongoing basis. And it is important that you know if you are in a buyer's or seller's market when you decide to sell your home.

The importance of knowing that information is tied to how you can more effectively **negotiate a deal** that will work for you and your family. When negotiating a sales contract always be aware of "time constraints" as they play an important role in any negotiation–and even more when buying and/or selling real estate.

The **offer price** and **contingencies** in the contract is key to a fair sale and should be entered into with the assistance of a loan officer and highly competent real estate agent who knows the market—generally speaking.

If you are selling your home and you own it outright, there are many options that are available including creative financing.

Always realize that a cash offer is not always the best offer as it does not always give you the most negotiating power when you are receiving an offer from a buyer!

You can accept a cash offer with a higher earnest money down payment and a shorter due diligence period to close in a timelier manner when you are in a seller's market and as the seller(s) you are receiving multiple offers on your property.

Generally, you want to be prepared to have the buyer pay the closing costs (they are usually low because no lender is involved) when you are presented with a cash offer.

The adage that "cash is KING" holds true for real estate purchasing and if buyers are competing against several cash buyers, your odds of receiving an offer that is acceptable to you goes up if financing is not required and you net the proceeds that you desire.

When financing is obtained to purchase your home, you will have to ensure that the buyer has a firm loan commitment and the financing contingency in the offer contract can be met and further negotiate the closing costs.

As a seller you should be aware that there are **mandatory seller closing costs** and there are closing costs that can be negotiated out with lenders and/or negotiated to be paid by the buyer(s) or seller(s) in many free market states and countries.

In a "buyer's market" you will have less flexibility in the offer you accept as there will be an abundance of homes on the market that may fit buyer's needs and if an offer is not accepted by a seller the buyer can move along to another similar property that is on the market.

Cash offers would normally be less prevalent in a buyer's market.

As a seller you (and your agent) want to control the negotiating process so that you can maximize the transaction to your advantage, but also make it a winning situation for the buyer(s) as well.

Your end goal is to "close on the property" and receive the net proceeds that you desire and at the same time make the sale of your home a win–win for all parties involved. It is important that you select an agent that is effective at negotiating and utilizing contingencies as they are both critical to your home selling success.

By being aware of the new trends in real estate and using the practical **negotiating tips** above when you anticipate selling your next home–you will put yourself in winning position whether you desire to sell a newly built home on your lot or a resale home. By utilizing the above process, you can be successful in the current economy or at a date well into the future, and whether you are selling in a buyer's or seller's market.

In **Chapter 1**, and throughout this book we will go over how you can use the "power of preparation" to make the selling of your home an enjoyable endeavor, and one that truly serves your and your family's best long-term objectives as it relates to a successful period after your home ownership ends or starts over at a new destination.

It is very important that you get your home ready for the market, thus ensuring that the selling of your home is a more enjoyable experience and one that serves your and your family's best long-term interest.

Chapter 1 Preparation— The Key to Your Successful Home Sale
(what you need to do to get your home ready for the market)

When selling your home be sure to consider the property condition. If you are selling the home yourself or using an agent you may have to provide home buyers a **property disclosure statement** that tells them the age, condition and whether household appliances and window treatments—or other items will remain with the home upon purchase.

When you are preparing your home for sale pay particular attention to the curb appeal of your home, the condition and age of the siding on the house, the condition and age of the gutters, soffits and overhang, the condition and age of the water heater, the condition and age of the heating and air conditioners, the condition and age of the roof, the age of the house (electrical problems usually occur after 20 years or so) and the plumbing system.

On the inside pay attention to the condition of walls, flooring, ceilings, ceiling fans, lighting, ventilation—and be especially alert for plumbing leaks—particularly in areas where water enters and exits the house.

Are the floors and walls level to you or can you immediately notice that they are out of balance? Make sure there are no visible signs of water entering the house from the roof area.

Also make sure you are aware of all **environmental concerns** (more on that in **Chapter 4**) in and around your home and address those concerns on the front end before your property goes on the market. Mold, Radon, Lead-Based Paints, and other concerns "that you are aware of" must be addressed prior to selling your home—not after!

If the amenities and social spots that potential buyers like are a long drive away—you need to factor that into your selling decision and asking price as well!

Keep in mind that all the above are preliminary steps that you need to take prior to placing your home on the market. If you are in position to do so, a home sale pre-inspection may be a wise choice so that you can address needed repairs on the front end, thereby leading to a smoother closing!

If you decide to use an inspector prior to putting your property on the market—be sure to have the home inspected by a **"qualified home inspector"** and consider the money spent (normally $350—$550— but can vary depending on the type house and where you live) as you can avoid putting your home on the market in a selling condition that is not up to market standards.

On this page and those that follow I will share helpful tips that can help prevent you from getting into a difficult real estate situation that is not in your best interest.

As a real estate professional and financial planner with over 20 years' experience, I have gathered and formulated these tips over many years to help consumers make home buying and home selling decisions that are good for THEM.

RESIDENTIAL REAL ESTATE TIPS

Seller Tips

Price your home right the first time

CURB APPEAL:

- Maximize curb appeal by trimming up and landscaping outside

- Make sure bushes, shrubs and trees are trimmed
- Make sure plants are trimmed and flower beds are weeded and mulched
- Make sure lawn is free from weeds and debris, trimmed, edged and cut
- Plant flowers, shrubs, and trees at least 12 inches from your house. Plant flowers, shrubs and trees with the mature size (maximum size) in mind and plant them further from the house based on expected maturity size
- Sweep all walkways, patios, and decks
- Mow and green up your grass with fertilizer
- First impressions are lasting impressions
- The longer your property sits on the market the less likely it is to sell at or near asking price so it is important to get these tips implemented before your property goes on the market.
- Make sure roof is clear of moss, debris and obstructions.
- Make sure the gutters are secure and clean
- Make sure windows and shutters are clean and in good repair
- Make sure siding is clean and secure
- Make sure that there is no peeled paint inside or out
- Make sure doors and hinges are clean and oiled

INSIDE APPEARANCE:

- Use neutral paint colors inside (touch-up where necessary)
- Neutral colors are easier to sell
- Each room should be clean of clutter
- Each room should be well lighted and free of odors
- Make sure you open drapes or shades to brighten room
- Make sure you keep toys, shoes, clothing and other inappropriate objects off the floor
- Make sure you clean your carpet—replace if necessary

- Make sure bathroom and kitchen is especially clean—eliminate clutter
- Make sure you keep trash to a minimum inside
- If your home needs work—do it to maximize sales price
- Make sure potential buyer is pre-qualified (or preferably pre-approved) for a home loan
- Make sure you get pre-qualified (or for more bargaining power pre-approved) before you start your next home search—unless, of course you intend to pay cash or you plan on renting
- Make sure you dust furniture and clean all windows
- Make sure you turn off TV or better yet don't be around when your home is being shown as most real estate agents and potential buyers are uncomfortable when the seller is present.
- Make sure you keep pets out of the way—preferably outside when house is being shown
- Realize that the first offer you get will normally be your best offer—however use your best judgement
- Make sure rooms are freshly painted and bright (neutral colors are usually best)
- Make sure light switches and covers are clean
- Make sure screens are repaired and cleaned
- Make sure chandeliers and glass covers are clean
- Make sure carpets have been professionally cleaned or replaced with neutral carpets

Depending on your home and your market area—it may be wise to have rooms staged for maximum appearance and space!

- Make sure clutter is removed
- Try to ensure that closets appear as large as possible (Remove items and store at another location if need be)
- Make sure you remove all clutter, garbage, and boxes

- Make sure you remove family photos, mementos, knickknacks, and personalized items
- Make sure you repair leaky faucets
- Make sure that the bathrooms and kitchens are especially clean. Clear any excess items so the rooms appear as large as possible
- Make sure you fix or replace worn or damaged tile, countertops, doorknobs, bathroom grout, lamps, lampshades, light switches/covers etcetera
- Make sure you replace any worn entry rugs or door mats.
- Make sure you check for odors, water stains and the like and correct
- Make sure cupboards, closets and pantry area is neat
- Organization and cleanliness give the potential home buyer a feeling that the rest of the house was well cared for

More Seller Tips...

- Make sure you install new bulbs outside and in
- Make sure you check bricks and pavers for cracks—replace them and reset any that are loose
- Make sure you patch worn or cracked asphalt or cement in the driveway and walkway
- Make sure you edge grass and remove weeds that may have grown over driveway and walkway
- Make sure you repaint the front door and freshen up chipped and peeling paint trim
- Make sure you clean and polish the brass on the doorknobs and locks, replace them if needed
- Make sure you replace any cracked/broken glass panes and missing window screens
- Make sure you clean out gutters and downspouts

- Make sure your mailbox is upright, steady, and has a desirable look
- Realize that a side or back entry garage will usually do better at resale than a front entry garage

PRIOR TO THE SHOWING:

- Open all the drapes and curtains to maximize lighting and spaciousness
- Turn on all lights, even in the daytime
- Turn on soft relaxing background music—if you will be present
- Ensure that bathrooms and other rooms are clean
- Scent all rooms with vanilla or another fresh pleasing smell
- Remove all pets!!!

AT THE SHOWING:

In today's world, it is wise to be cautious. Make sure you know who is coming to your home! Beyond that, when the doorbell rings for showings you should politely answer the door. Once you have identified the agent you should then excuse yourself and go outside or at the very least not be in the same area as your potential buyers and agent.

If you remain nearby the potential buyer will feel uncomfortable and not spend the time that they should looking at your house. Additionally, they will not feel comfortable looking into the cupboards, closets, attics etcetera, and asking their agent questions.

REMAIN FLEXIBLE:

Whether you are a home buyer or a home seller, time is of the essence. In simple definition, any delay, reasonable or not, slight or not, may mean the loss of a sale or a cancellation of a contract. Remain flexible on when agents can show your property.

Additionally, keep in mind that contingencies, specific moving dates, and similar items that you hear of in contracts can often have undesirable effects. Consult your attorney and real estate agent. Be ready to negotiate whether utilizing a realtor or not.

It is often wise to use a real estate agent, as navigating the increasingly complex real estate transaction is much easier when buyers and sellers have professional help.

Buyer Tips:

Even though you are now seriously considering the selling of your home, you may also have a need to purchase a home after your sale. If you decide to purchase again, you too should always have an agent represent you as there is normally no cost associated when you are a buyer, and an agent can provide invaluable insight and potentially help you save thousands.

It is very important that you never go into a new home subdivision without an agent. If you do, at least inform the sales rep that you have an agent and get one prior to submitting your offer. If you say no, they assume you don't, and they represent the builder's best interest—NOT YOURS.

Also realize that potential buyers of your home may also utilize the preceding tips and those that follow when analyzing your property that you have that will go on the market.

- Know what type of siding is on the house and the year it was applied
- Defective siding is not uncommon for homes built in the 1990's
- Make sure the house does not have lead based paint
- Does the house have Polybutylene piping

- Be sure you know the age (how old) of the <u>water heater</u>, furnace, and air conditioner
- Make sure you know how old the roof is
- Make sure you know how old the deck is
- Has the house been regularly treated for termites
- Does the house meet your minimum needs based on your price range
- Is the proximity to your job, schools and recreation appropriate for you
- Have you been pre-approved for your home loan
- Will you have a 6-month emergency fund after you purchase your home
- Have you fairly compared what you are considering paying versus the actual sold properties in the same subdivision or area
- Do you have a <u>quality code certified, licensed, and bonded home inspector</u>
- Make sure there are no big cracks in masonry, brick, and concrete
- Make sure you look for water stains or evidence of previous water stains on the ceilings, under sinks, and any area where water enters or exits the house
- Make sure you consider a home warranty
- Radon tests are a good idea in many areas in the United States
- A termite bond retreatment repair bond is generally a good investment
- Make sure you always purchase "Buyers Title Insurance" at closing

In the purchase of your home consider rates offered by Mortgage Lenders and Mortgage Brokers

- Make sure you use caution when considering the purchase of a home on a main road
- Realize that a house on a corner lot is not always best
- Make sure you are aware of utility easements
- Something of concern—be sure to put it in writing in the sales contract
- A creek or pond in a yard is not always a good thing
- A side entry garage is not always a good thing
- If you purchase in a lake community–at times of drought the lake may recede and you may have an unsightly view
- Know who the closing attorney represents. In many areas they may not represent YOU even though you may think they are
- Make sure you avoid dual agency when purchasing your home
- Make sure that you are aware of past flooding in the area and never buy in a designated flood zone
- Has the house been updated
- Are there any upgrades that I can make
- Determine your wants and needs before you begin your home search
- Realize that your wants and needs may have to be altered depending on your loan qualification and area
- Are you qualified to do any repairs or renovations
- Location, location, location affects current and future value and your lifestyle—know grading on the lot
- Know if quality schools and strong city or county management is in place
- Know how long you plan to live in your new house (within reason—life can be unpredictable)
- Know that it is your responsibility to determine if there are undesirable environmental or safety concerns in the area that you are considering moving to

Unless you are in a distressed selling situation you want to ensure that you prepare your home for selling on the front end—prior to putting your property on the market—where possible.

Are you willing to accept a 203k loan or other rehab loan from a buyer and get reduced proceeds if you are unable to do the needed repairs prior to putting your home on the market?

You want to ask and answer probing questions on the front end—not after you put your property on the market for sale.

Now that you have a meaningful understanding of the preparation that is needed to get your home ready for sale—lets now look at **Personal Financial Statements** and see how your effective understanding and use of them can be of benefit to you and your family prior to and after selling your home!

Having the ability to utilize personal financial statements to your advantage, prior to putting your property on the market is an important step for preparing for the future success that you desire—and deserve!

47

Chapter 2 How to Use Personal Financial Statements to Your Benefit When Selling Your Home

There are many different types of financial statements available that can help you get a better picture of where you stand financially.

By preparing in advance for a successful home sale you will distinguish yourself from the crowd and you will be in position to use "personal financial statements" in the manner that they should be used—for your and your family's greater benefit!

There are many different types of financial statements available that can help you get a better picture of where you stand financially.

A <u>Personal Cash Flow Statement (Budget)</u> is a statement that reflects your income and expenses on a monthly basis.

By properly utilizing this statement prior to purchasing and/or selling your home—it can help you determine if home ownership is appropriate for you at this time, or whether staying where you are and saving—and/or pursuing other options are your best choice.

A <u>personal cash flow statement</u> helps determine how liquid you are and is a good barometer in determining your ability to meet your future financial obligations.

In addition, by doing a pre-sale and a post-sale cash flow statement (cash flow income and expenses analysis before and after you have sold your home) you can get a realistic picture of how you can enjoy your life after selling your home.

Furthermore, you will know the cash that you will have left over <u>(discretionary income)</u> after your future housing (or rental) expenses and all of your other debts have been analyzed.

Remember, it is best that you do both the pre and post-sale cash flow analysis **"prior to"** and after selling your home. Even if you don't exactly know your future housing and other expenses, it is best to use projected realistic expenses to ensure that you have no future surprises.

If the financial picture that you get in the pre-sale and post-sale cash flow analysis is not to your liking, you are in the position to not proceed with the sale and sell later if you desire—once you are in a better financial position.

A _Personal Income Statement_ **is a statement that analyzes and summarizes your income and expenses over an interval of time.**

An Income and Expense Statement presents a summary of your income and expenses during an interval of time, usually one year.

By subtracting the expenses from your income, you will come up with your discretionary cash flow (money available to you after all expenses are accounted for). This is money that you can use for enjoyment, debt reduction, additional savings, gifts or whatever else you may desire.

If you use the discretionary cash flows to reduce debt or to save, your balance sheet ratios will improve and hence your net worth will increase, which should always be your annual goal.

Your "discretionary income" is income that you can spend any way that you like—after your fixed and variable expenses have been paid.

Your "discretionary expenses" are your luxuries or expenses over which you have total control as to whether you want to incur them or not. For example—vacations, entertainment, gifts, and the like.

A **Personal Balance Sheet Statement** is a statement that analyzes your assets and liabilities at a single point in time.

The balance sheet is a listing of assets, liabilities, and net worth that outlines your resources and shows how those resources were obtained or financed.

The statement is a particular snapshot of your finances at a particular point in time (the date of the statement). Many third parties (banks, lenders etcetera) utilized the balance sheet in the past when deciding to grant certain credit.

Today it would be used in conjunction with your personal income statement and cash flow statement if you were to seek a loan of a certain type for certain credit.

Your Net Worth is the amount of wealth or equity you have in owned assets.

Your net worth is calculated by taking the difference between your total assets and your total liabilities.

Regardless of your assets and your liabilities the statement must always balance.

In simple form Assets minus Liabilities = Net Worth.

A balance sheet will give you a good idea of your financial condition if you are organized and want to totally take control of your finances.

A Personal Balance Sheet Statement will show you whether you hit your targeted goals and show you if you fell short.

By preparing the balance sheet in advance you can use it for budgeting and/or projections and when used in conjunction with your cash flow statement and income statement, it can give you a much clearer picture of your financial future.

By being able to see your future more clearly you will be in a much better position than you were to make decisions that are good for you and your family.

A **Statement of Net Worth** is a statement that tells essentially what you are worth after your assets and liabilities have been analyzed.

Your "Net Worth Statement" is a much better metric than simply what your income is or what you appear to own and appear to owe.

Your annual goal should always be to increase your net worth.

A major factor in increasing your net worth is the proper buying and selling of your home!

The Statement of Net Worth is derived from the Balance Sheet.

You can use your personal cash flow statement or personal budget, personal income statement, and personal balance sheet in conjunction with your net worth statement to get a better idea of your overall financial health.

By knowing your financial situation up front you can plan for your future more effectively and get a realistic picture of how you can enjoy life and get the pleasures of life that you know you deserve.

Also, by knowing your financial position after your home purchase **(by doing this analysis on the front end)** you will know your financial situation after your projected home sale.

You will know what your discretionary (money left after all your monthly expenses have been paid) income is and know prior to purchasing or selling if you can continue doing the things you like to do—or do additional things that you are not doing at this time!

In short, financial statements can help you plan better when you have adequate financial information in easy-to-understand statements.

The financial statements, however, are only as good as the accuracy of the data inputted!

Therefore, you want to be sure that your income and expenses are as accurate as possible, "and" your assets and liabilities are as accurate as possible.

The real value of the above financial statements will be seen years down the road in the improved living conditions for you and your family.

The above financial statements are an aid to sound financial management and not a substitute for sound financial management.

The real key is do you have the proper motivation inside to apply the information derived from the financial analysis to move in the **right direction** to improve your life and that of your family's?

By applying the information properly, it will benefit you and your family the most.

You also want to use your expected future housing payment after you sell your home, your monthly debt (payments of one year or more such as credit card debt, student loan debt, car loans etcetera) and your monthly income to determine if you are not purchasing your next home with a monthly payment that is too high.

You can go to the following website and quickly determine how to improve your credit and purchase your home with a monthly payment that will allow you to enjoy your purchase and meet your other household obligations:

http://www.the-best-atlanta-real-estate-advice.com

You already know the importance of mastering your credit so that you can purchase your new home and effectively manage your credit throughout your lifetime or during the period of your life that you desire to utilize credit.

You can round out and enhance your understanding of your finances by having the mindset to learn all you can about insurance, investments, taxes, emergency fund, education planning, estate planning/wills and retirement planning later, by visiting **TheWealthIncreaser.com** on a consistent basis once your time allows you to do so.

Now that you have a meaningful understanding of "Personal Financial Statements", and you know how they can be of substantial benefit to you and your family prior to your home sale—let us now look at the "home loan process" and "home selling process" in the **next few chapters** to see how you can make the sale of your home work for you—and not against you!

Chapter 3 Home Loan & Closing Costs Revisited

After you sell your home you may need to purchase a move-up home or refinance—you can go to quickenloans.com or lendingtree.com along with local mortgage lenders in your area to determine what loan will best suit you and your family. You can compare closing costs, APR's and Par rates to determine what loan will best serve your and your family's long-term interests.

As a current homeowner and someone who has the goal of selling your home in the most advantageous way, you already know something about closing costs if you purchased your home that you are considering for sale using financing.

In this chapter we will revisit closing costs so that you will know what the buyer of your home will go through and refresh your mind so that you know what to expect if you are moving up (or down) and you will use financing in the purchase of your next home.

Key facts:

Home Loan Closing Costs are generally in the 3% range in many areas, however, keep in mind that it is also based on the amount that you borrow and local custom.

As a home purchaser you can negotiate to pay the closing costs, you can negotiate to have the seller pay the closing costs, or you can negotiate to split the closing costs.

*Basically, who pays the **closing costs** are negotiable. In the end it will be the purchaser who really pays the cost.*

Let's say you receive an offer of $200,000 to purchase your home from the buyer.

The seller owes $160,000 on his current loan. Closing Costs are $6,000 and the real estate commission (in which the seller pays) is $12,000 and the seller agrees to pay closing costs. The seller would net $22,000 under this scenario.

If the seller liked the offer and the net proceeds he would accept.

Keep in mind that it is the $200,000 offer price that actually paid the closing costs and the seller netted $22,000 which was the seller's goal.

If the seller needed to net $24,000, he would possibly agree to pay 2% of the closing costs and that would net him/her the $24,000 that he/she needed.

Likewise, the seller could choose to reduce the price and have the seller pay all the closing costs, Increase the price, and split the costs, or negotiate still further on the sales price or other areas of the contract until mutual agreement could be reached.

Closing Costs include several charges that are a result of your new loan and include the following which are the most common.

Legitimate fees are listed below:

- Appraisal Fee—On an average metro Atlanta area house the fee is $300 to $500. For other types of property, it could be higher. The fee will vary depending on your area

- Lender's Title Insurance Fee—The lender will purchase lender's title insurance to help protect against errors in title or past ownership error that may arise.

You must purchase a separate policy to protect your own interest!

I strongly recommend title insurance to all home buyer's that I represent—and you too, should strongly consider getting your own title policy for future protection in title disputes.

The coverage usually cannot exceed the purchase price, so if you have a title dispute years down the road, after the value of your property has doubled, your maximum payoff would still be the price you purchased the property for.

Disputes in title are rare, but they can and do occur. For several hundred dollars you can buy a policy to protect yourself and your family from potential title disputes.

- Intangibles Tax Fee—**In Georgia, where our office is located, we have intangibles tax**

The intangibles tax on a new loan is $3 per thousand or 3/10th of 1% in Georgia—so a 200,000-house loan would cost you $600.

There appear to be no logical reason to have this other than a big money generator for the State of Georgia.

- Transfer Tax Fee—Tax Service Fee is a tax for transfer of ownership

- State Tax or State Stamps—Fee charged by some states in a real estate transaction.

- Recording Fee—Fee to publicly record documents so that the world knows you own the property or have an ownership interest in the property.

- Attorney's Fee—It is usually about $600 or more on a typical closing. If you have an unusual closing such as a simultaneous closing expect to pay more. Fees also varies by location

- Loan Origination Fee—This is usually the highest amount paid in most closings other than real estate commission which is usually paid by the seller.

The lender normally takes the loan application, assembles the loan package, coordinates the appraisal and closing, and they must be paid for their services.

- Loan Discount Fee—This fee is paid to buy the loan down. One discount point is 1% of the loan amount—and it may buy the loan down about a quarter of one percent.

- Miscellaneous—Some miscellaneous fees are legitimate; however, many are questionable and/or junk fees.

Legitimate fees are listed above and if they are on your closing cost document, initial fees estimate, good faith estimate, loan estimate, truth-in-lending statement etcetera—they are to be expected!

However, the fees listed below are questionable and you should use caution to determine if you want to pay them based on your current finances and credit position:

- Discount Fee
- Underwriting Fee
- Warehouse Fee
- Creative Fees
- Duplicate Fees
- Up-charges

Junk fees are often utilized by lenders and/or loan officers to pad their earnings and they are listed below:

- Administrative Fee
- Application Fee
- Appraisal Review Fee
- Ancillary Fee
- Courier Fee
- Documentation Preparation Fee
- Document Review Fee
- Email Fee
- Processing Fee
- Title Review Fee
- Settlement Fee

- Survey Fee

If you are in a **"strong credit position"** and/or are putting a large down payment down—an experienced lender should reduce or eliminate these fees because they know that you have a strong credit or cash position and they know that you can go elsewhere and get a loan that does not include those junk fees.

If more than four junk fees or junk fees that you don't like are included you should negotiate them out, have them reduced or consider crossing the loan company off your list of potential lenders.

NOTE: If you anticipate purchasing your home in a conventional manner (from a home seller) it may be wise for you to get **"pre-approved"** on the front end.

By choosing among 3 or 4 lenders (remember don't give out your social security number or have your credit pulled at this point) and comparison shopping—you can decide which company to choose for your home loan and then get pre-approved prior to house hunting if it is in your best interest to do so!

*Be sure to get your magic marker or pen out and go line by line over the above fees **on your Loan Estimate (discussed in more detail later in this chapter—also once known as the Good Faith Estimate)** to see if you want to pay the questionable or junk fees above **so** that you can reduce the overall cost of your loan!*

By being in a strong credit position you can "politely" ask the loan officer to remove the fees and if they don't, you can move on to a lender who will not only remove the fees but will also offer you a better package deal with a lower APR and the same or a better interest rate!

Truth-In-Lending Statement:

Required by Law—it is neither a contract nor commitment to lend but it will state the APR, the finance charge, the amount financed, and the total number of payments.

In a nutshell the federal Truth-in-Lending Act - or "TILA" for short – requires that borrowers receive written disclosures about important terms of credit **before** they are legally bound to pay the loan.

The initial **Truth-In-Lending-Disclosure** or **TRID (Good Faith Estimate)** as it was commonly named was replaced by a **Loan Estimate** in 2015. The **Closing Disclosure** also came into effect, and it replaced the final **Truth-In-Lending-Disclosure** that lenders, real estate agents and closing attorneys had become familiar with for many years.

The Loan Estimate and/or Closing Disclosure will also state if there is a pre-payment penalty either partial or full.

If partial, you may be entitled to a refund of finance charge. If "may have a penalty" is checked that means, there will be one. The Closing Disclosure will also state if the loan is assumable or not.

On the Loan Estimate be alert for:

- Proper rate calculations
- Filing fees
- Pre-payment penalty (hard or soft)
- Loan balance * 0.80 * interest rate/2 = pre-payment penalty
- Refund of finance charge
- Loan assumption
- Be aware that statement is an estimate only

- No credit life, or credit disability is checked (it is normally best to purchase life insurance or disability insurance in the open market—however, the decision as to whether you want to purchase it through your mortgage company is ultimately up to you)

Loan Estimate (previously called Good Faith Estimate):

The **TR**uth **I**n Lending **D**isclosure **(TRID)** contains important information for any homebuyer who is considering taking out a mortgage loan. The **LE** breaks down the various costs associated with a home purchase into line items. The information is like that of the GFE; however, the format is more easily understood.

Loan Estimates are required to include estimates for:

*Type of loan, such as conventional or FHA

*Interest rate for the loan

*Total monthly payments, including breakdowns by year if it is an ARM loan

*Balloon payment if applicable

*Total closing costs

*Property taxes

*Insurance costs

*Pre-payment penalties, if applicable

Lenders must include certain information in a prominent place on the first page of the three-page document, including the total monthly payment and estimated cash to close. This requirement aims to make the most pertinent information readily available and obvious to consumers to enhance their decision making and make comparison loan shopping easier.

It's important to note that a loan estimate is not the same as an official loan approval!

An estimate is just that, an educated guess about what the lender predicts your terms would look like. After you provide more details about your income and debts, you may see some changes to the terms.

It's in the best interest of a lender to make the estimate as accurate as possible, as they know a borrower may walk away if the terms change drastically between an estimate and an official offer.

The Good Faith Estimate is still required by law for reverse mortgages and <u>this document will give you an estimate of all the costs contained in closing your loan.</u>

It is wise to ask for your loan estimate "<u>before</u>" you make loan application. It does not make good financial sense to apply for a loan (and obligate yourself financially) before you know what your costs are.

Ask for a written guarantee that the final costs will not vary by more than 8%-10% of the amount stated on the Loan Estimate.

Also, if you have a written commitment, you can compare it to other lenders (you should have 3 or 4 lenders or mortgage brokers) so that you can put yourself in position to choose the loan that is best for you and your family.

Did you know that the **Homeowner Protection Act of 1998** gives consumers the right to cancel **Private Mortgage Insurance** (insurance that is required if you put less than 20% down)—if certain conditions are met?

It is also important that you know that you can cancel your escrow account on your mortgage payment according to your lender guidelines when you reach a certain equity position, however you must ask your lender to do so. You must then directly pay your taxes and homeowner's insurance yourself.

Other questions to ask the loan officer:

If interest rates go down between the original Loan Estimate (LE) and the lock-in period—who should benefit?

The client, or the loan officer, or both?

Asking intelligent questions is the best way to communicate that you are a savvy consumer, and you won't be easily taken advantage of!

Always state (and be true to it) to loan officer that you have all your paperwork handy and will be easy to work with.

Ask for a statement (or guarantee) in writing that says that the mortgage company's final cost will not vary by no more than 10%—at the most.

The loan estimate and good faith estimate documents share many details and can help borrowers more easily understand and compare their options before proceeding with a mortgage application.

The **Loan Estimate** helps provide borrowers the ability to more effectively comparison shop a mortgage.

The Good Faith Estimate **(GFE)** was designed to encourage consumers to shop and then compare fees from various lenders <u>before choosing a mortgage</u> provider. Its original purpose was to help consumers understand what services they could shop for—so they not only received the lowest interest rate and best terms but saved significantly on closing costs, as well—and the **Loan Estimate** is designed to enhance the process even more for potential home buyers.

Again, the **GFE** has been replaced by the **Loan Estimate**, and the **HUD-1** by the **Closing Disclosure**, however many veterans in the industry still used the old terminology.

If you purchased a home after October 3, 2015, you should have received a Loan Estimate and a Closing Disclosure!

The new document is very similar to the original. Let's further look at what they cover so you have an even clearer understanding.

- In Closing Disclosures, fees can't increase from the estimate more than the tolerance level of that category unless there is an allowed trigger event.

HUD provides specific criteria for what constitutes a complete loan application.

It should include:

- The borrower's name, income, and Social Security number
- The property address
- The estimated value of the property
- The loan amount
- Anything else the lender deems necessary or that was agreed upon with the buyer

The Loan Estimate is now standardized and lists services for which you are allowed to shop. You may not be able to shop for an appraisal fee or a credit report fee, but you could be able to shop for a land survey and title insurance. Lenders will vary in their requirements and what are considered closing costs will vary from lender to lender.

All lenders must provide consumers with the exact same document. Loan charges, third-party fees, and other costs must be displayed uniformly.

The older **Good Faith Estimate** had no such uniformity requirements.

The **Loan Estimate** encourages consumers to shop by issuing a standardized loan estimate in a specific time frame.

Furthermore, HUD states that prior to the issuance of a loan estimate, lenders can only charge potential borrowers a fee to cover the expense of a credit report.

The relatively low cost of credit reports ($20–$40) results in a consumer's ability to comparison shop among many lenders at a minimal cost.

Your "comparison of home loans" has been made much easier than in the past as the process is less cumbersome. Therefore, as a potential borrower you want to compare the rates and fees among several lenders if you have a desire to obtain the best or optimal rate possible on your home loan.

The Closing Disclosure

Lenders are held accountable for their quotes. Prior to October 3, 2015, each section in the **GFE** would directly correspond to a section of the **HUD-1**, which you would receive upon closing.

This was a standardized document that listed every expense involved in a real estate or refinancing transaction.

The **HUD-1** has been replaced by the **Closing Disclosure**, which designates fee tolerance levels. What this means is that a fee cannot increase from the **Loan Estimate** more than the tolerance level set for that fee category, unless there is a permitted triggering event.

There are **three different tolerance categories** to be aware of—0%, 10%, and no tolerance.

- The zero-tolerance category includes fees for the services for the creditor, broker, or any business affiliates of anyone involved in the process. These fees cannot change.

- The 10%-tolerance category allows for a 10% variance of recording fees, title documents, and services for which the buyer must shop from an approved list, such as a home inspector.

- The no-limit-tolerance category allows for unlimited changes in fees for services not required by the creditor or not on the creditor's approved list, such as a septic inspection or a property survey. This category also includes prepaid interest and any property taxes and insurance paid into escrow.

In summary, the **Loan Estimate** improves on the older **Good Faith Estimate** by enabling homebuyers to compare loan options and ensure their final loan fees conform closely to their original quote. Both the **Loan Estimate** and **Closing Disclosure** documents were designed to hold realtors, brokers, and lenders accountable and provide greater transparency for you—the consumer.

By understanding and applying the information in this chapter for your greater benefit on your next home loan or refinance, you put yourself and your family in control of the closing costs and you avoid having the closing costs (mortgage lender) control you and your family!

In **Chapter 4** we will look at environmental concerns that you need to be aware of so that you can ensure a more successful sale of your home.

Chapter 4 Environmental Concerns

In this chapter you will learn why it is so important to know what is in the environment in and around the home that you are about to put on the market for sale.

It is important that you consider the environmental aspect of living when you are in the home selling process.

That means that it is your responsibility to reasonably determine if the home that you are considering for sale—does not contain lead, mold, radon, or other environmental contaminants in your home or if it does and you know it you must disclose it.

It also means that you must do your due diligence ahead of your future move and ensure that the immediate radius in which you plan on moving to is also free of environmental concerns and other concerns that you may have.

Is the air quality appropriate? Are the waterways and drinking water at an acceptable level? Are there noise factors that I need to know? Are there sex offender registrants in the area that I live in or plan to move to?

In short—you need to ensure on the front end that the house and the area that you are considering for your move after you sell your current home is at an acceptable level from an environmental and safety standpoint!

Do You Know the Difference between Green and Sustainable Building?

Although often used interchangeably, the terms green and sustainable are not one and the same. Both terms do include the ideas of recycling and reusing, managing waste, and overall energy conservation.

Green Building

Generally, a green building is a structure designed and built to use less energy and promote healthier living, and it is usually constructed with materials that are recycled or made from renewable raw materials.

Sustainable Building

A sustainable building is a structure that actually produces the energy required to operate the building.

This is known as building to zero-energy standards.

Sustainable buildings and sustainable communities are designed to lessen the dependency on fossil fuels in homes and in transportation and workplaces.

Sustainable Building Concepts

Many consumers are unfamiliar with the differences among concepts of building green, sustainable building, energy efficiency, and renewable energy.

It will increasingly become the responsibility of your real estate agent to understand these concepts—and to aid you in making informed choices—relating to the purchase of both residential and commercial buildings.

However, the ultimate responsibility resides with you—so be sure to do your due diligence on the front end!

Sustainability is all about minimizing the environmental impact of building houses, buildings, and communities. Early planning **on** individual buildings and entire communities are needed to integrate all processes into sustainable building of homes, buildings, and communities.

Sustainability is directed toward the five following concepts:

1) Optimizing the use of the sun in energy choices

2) Improving indoor air quality

3) Responsible land use

4) Building high-performance and moisture-resistant buildings

5) Making wise use of natural resources

Earthcraft Design

EarthCraft House is a voluntary builder program dedicated to energy-efficient and environmentally friendly home design and construction.

EarthCraft House-certified builders must meet the program's stringent requirements in heating/ventilation/air conditioning systems, ductwork, attic insulation, erosion control, exterior cladding, and window and door openings, among others.

Although builders have flexibility in selecting the EarthCraft approaches best suited to their homes, they must submit a worksheet stating which measures they plan to incorporate.

These include but are not limited to site planning, energy-efficient building envelope and systems, energy-efficient appliances and lighting, resource-efficient design and **building materials**, waste management, indoor air quality, and efficient indoor water use.

The worksheet is detailed and must be verified by an EarthCraft House inspector.

An Earthcraft certified home will normally lower your energy costs and do less damage to the environment—in some cases significantly—therefore if you are building your new home be sure to consider the Earthcraft or Energy Efficient design from the outset.

Do You Know What the Energy Certifications Are?

It is important that you realize that various certification programs are being developed to help you understand the effect of the choices to be made regarding energy that you use.

Among the certifications that you must be aware of are:

1) Energy Star® and

2) Leadership in Energy and Environmental Design (LEED)

Energy Efficiency

In proportion to its percentage of the world's population, the United States uses more energy than any other economy. The United States represents about 5% of the world population but uses about 25% of the world's energy.

This is becoming an issue among the underdeveloped nations who, as their population grows, will require more energy usage.

Oil, coal, and natural gas are being used up at ever-increasing rates. The challenge for builders of houses and commercial and industrial buildings, as well as for those involved in the design of planned communities, is increased energy conservation.

Energy conservation in building should start with reducing the demand for energy and choosing appliances that use less energy, especially energy with fossil fuel as its source, with the ultimate goal of using no energy from fossil fuels.

Renewable energy, which is generally considered energy produced by non-fossil fuel, comes to us in the form of solar, wind, and geothermal energy.

Today, most electricity is produced through fossil fuels, and a stated goal in the move toward energy efficiency is to entirely convert the production of electricity to renewable resources.

Reuse—is a term applied to using a product more than once— either for the same purpose or for a new purpose.

Examples of reuse in today's society are the following:

- Refillable glass bottles
- Washable diapers instead of disposable diapers
- Refillable ink cartridges for printers
- Re-furbishable electronic products
- Reusable Plastic Products

Recycling is the concept of taking a product, breaking it down, and reassembling it into a different product.

Recycling is different from simply reusing the product.

Recycling reduces the need for landfills and for creating more new material, which reduces the need to use energy.

Glass, paper, aluminum, asphalt, iron, and even concrete can be recycled. Most residential communities have developed recycling strategies to conserve energy.

Always Realize That Environmental Concerns Could Have an Impact on Your Insurance

As we are all aware, homeowner's insurance policy costs have been increasing, and some insurance companies have totally withdrawn from issuing homeowner's insurance.

The potential of costly litigation related to mold is a contributing factor to the increase in premiums and in insurance companies' decision to stop writing homeowner policies!

The insurance industry has created a database that tracks the claims filed on a home during the past seven years through the Comprehensive Loss Underwriting Exchange (CLUE), and it uses this claim history to justify increased rates or even to deny reissuing the homeowner's insurance policy—even on houses that had water damage <u>before</u> you moved in.

**Therefore, be sure to check the <u>CLUE report</u>
—on a home that you are considering purchasing!**

Many homeowners who have filed claims relating to water damage have found the insurance companies unwilling to renew their policies at the next renewal date.

Always Realize That There is the Real Potential For Health Issues Related To Environmental Concerns!

In the following paragraphs some of the more common issues that affect consumers that you should be particularly aware of will be addressed!

Mold & Mildew

Mold and mildew in real estate can cause health problems. Molds produce allergens (substances that can cause allergic reactions), irritants, and in some cases, potentially toxic substances.

Inhaling or touching mold or mold spores may cause allergic reactions in sensitive individuals.

Allergic responses include hay fever–type symptoms, such as sneezing, runny nose, red eyes, and skin rash. Allergic reactions to mold are common and can be immediate or delayed.

Molds can also cause asthma attacks in people with asthma who are allergic to mold.

In addition, mold exposure can irritate the eyes, skin, nose, throat, and lungs of both mold-allergic and non-allergic people.

If your home—or one that you are considering purchasing has suffered from flood damage—be sure to read the **FEMA Guide about Mold & Mildew!**

In addition, be sure to read the Basic Facts About Mold & Mildew that is provided from the CDC (Center for Disease Control)!

Government Issues Concerning Mold and Mildew

Parts of buildings that are tightly sealed and do not have adequate ventilation are prime areas where mold and mildew may be found.

Current construction practices may promote the growth of mold and mildew—in buildings that may be too tightly sealed—during construction.

Moisture enters buildings through roof leaks, furnaces that are not properly vented, and landscaping or gutters that cause water to gather and be directed toward the building.

The number of toxic mold and mildew cases filed in the courts has been increasing during recent years.

The courts have awarded settlements in these cases that in some instances have reached into millions of dollars. Consumers (you) as well as real estate agents—should expect the number of claims to rise as the awareness of the presence of mold and mildew increases.

In some states, real estate licensees are required to conduct a reasonably diligent visual inspection, and in others, many licensees conduct such an examination of the property even though not expressly required by law to do so.

Conditions observed during a visual inspection may include issues that could lead to mold problems.

A competent real estate agent should not speculate about whether these conditions may in fact indicate a mold problem—because an agent is generally not trained in such matters.

In every transaction, sellers should be encouraged to disclose any actual knowledge they have of mold problems on their properties.

Most sellers do not know whether their properties have mold problems!

If the seller(s) are aware of a mold problem, they should ask a competent expert to determine the extent of the mold present—and to recommend any corrective actions that are required to eliminate the mold issue.

In situations where your real estate agent notes red flags indicating the possibility of latent property defects, the buyer (you) should also be advised, in writing, that it may be prudent to contact a qualified expert to inspect the property and determine the nature of any problems—and what options for remediation exist.

Radon Gas

It is wise to have any home that you are considering for purchase— tested for high levels (dangerous) of radon gas.

There are remedies available to correct high levels of radon in a home so be sure to pursue them prior to closing on your home, or you may want to avoid purchasing a home with high radon levels.

Some areas of the country have higher levels than others. Radon is an odorless gas that comes from beneath the ground and can be at a dangerous level in some homes.

Be sure to read a <u>Citizens Guide to Radon</u> and <u>The Radon Fact Sheet</u>—prior to purchasing your home!

Lead-Based Paint

Homes built prior to 1978 have the potential to have lead-based paint—and disclosure is mandatory in most states for those who are selling homes that were built prior to 1978.

Be sure to read the <u>HUD (Housing & Urban Development) Pamphlet on Lead-Based Paint</u> and the <u>EPA (Environmental Protection Agency) Guide.</u>

In addition, be sure to read the <u>Lead Poisoning is Preventable Guide</u> that is also available from the EPA.

Final Thoughts on Environmental Concerns

Highly competent real estate licensees are expected to provide buyers and sellers the information they need to make major financial decisions related to the purchase or sale of residential, commercial or industrial real estate.

Be sure that the Real Estate agent that you select to represent you are aware of the ever-changing rules in the environmental arena.

The agent that you choose to represent you should diligently search out the training available so that they remain aware of the latest information on environmental concerns and they are aware of their—and buyers and sellers responsibilities—around energy conservation and environmental concerns.

The "real estate agent" that you choose to represent you should also provide you with additional resources about environmental concerns so that you can make a better-informed decision—whether you are a home buyer or a home seller.

In the end, you the seller (or buyer) should be proactive in ensuring that all environmental concerns are appropriately addressed whether inside or outside of the home that you will put on the market or the home and area that you are considering for your next move.

In **Chapter 5** we will look at the steps that you need to take to make your home purchase a more successful one so that you can have a conceptual understanding of the home selling process in more detail.

In **Chapter 6** you will be presented with what you need to know if you are considering selling your home without the assistance of a real estate agent (as a **For S**ale **B**y **O**wner).

Keep in mind that if you are in a distressed situation and you are considering selling your home as a short sale you will have additional considerations.

Chapter 5 Overview of the Home Selling Process

The home selling process begins well before you list your property for sale. You must ensure that your home is in selling condition prior to listing with an agent if you desire to maximize your return on your home investment.

You must choose an effective agent and one who knows how to get things done in a timely and efficient manner.

On this page and those that follow, I will share more about the home selling process so that you can get a conceptual overview of what is involved. However, as you read—keep in mind that all home selling situations are unique.

Purchasing and selling real estate can be complex and confusing if you are not properly prepared and informed about the process.

The complete selling process consists of the preparation that you have already done plus what you are about to read.

It starts with preliminary home seller preparation to post-closing in my opinion. A professional real estate agent should be concerned with more than just your ability to sell your home—they should also be concerned with your ability to get the needed funds from the sale and assist you in your next move in a way that you are satisfied.

Therefore, "preliminary pre-preparation" mentioned in the earlier chapters are a vital step. Don't skip this step, many home sellers do not prepare their property for sale appropriately and many fail to analyze their personal finances appropriately prior to putting their home on the market. Still others have no conceptual overview of the home selling process and the knowledge of the steps that are involved.

Don't let that be you!

The home selling process begins well before you put your home on the market and a buyer decides to place an offer on your home.

The preparation that you put into selling your home on the front end will pay great dividends on the back end if you do it the smart way.

I often have the potential home seller pull their credit from the three major credit bureaus and have them obtain their credit scores as well.

This gives the seller confidence that they are in control of their own financial destiny!

Although they may not see it now, this will help them start to take control of their financial affairs in a more forceful manner if they are not doing so already. Assuming their credit and credit scores are satisfactory, and **they plan on purchasing another home (**move-up home) their financial ratios (based on realistic projections) for their next purchase is analyzed.

A quick front end and back-end ratio analysis is then performed.

If their credit and credit score situation is unsatisfactory, they correct them (usually within 12 months) and we then move to the next step.

Assuming you have no bankruptcies, judgments, or other public record data on your report it can normally be cleaned up within 12 months if you have the right cash flow and you are disciplined in paying off outstanding debt and paying your revolving and installment accounts in a timely manner.

While working with seller's I try to implement a comprehensive strategy in their home selling pursuit.

Assuming all the above turns out to be positive I inform them of the home selling process in greater detail.

I then inform sellers of the advantages of getting a firm loan commitment from the buyer's lender early in the process.

Once the offer is accepted and a final sales price is negotiated, and terms are agreed to—the buyer performs an inspection (usually a professional inspector is hired) based on the time limits specified in the offer.

If there are problems of concern to the purchaser, we counter the offer and negotiate until a final sales price is agreed to. Once all contingencies are met the contract moves forward and the closing occurs.

Once the contract is accepted the buyer makes a formal application for the loan (unless buying with cash) and once the buyer receives the loan commitment letter (a contract between the borrower and the lender—the process moves forward.

Once the inspection is complete and repairs are negotiated the contract continues to move forward. If no agreement is reached the contract may become null and void.

Assuming the contract moves forward and closing approaches after the buyer receives their mortgage commitment, the attorney will submit a title insurance binder along with other legal paperwork required by the lender. Once everybody has signed off approval a closing date can be set.

Most Real estate closings are often exciting and stressful at the same time!

There are many legal papers being shuffled back and forth, as well as checks for large sums of money being exchanged among parties.

It is highly recommended that buyers do a final walk through of their home prior to closing to ensure that the condition is as stated by the terms of the contract.

The final walk through allows buyers to reconfirm the condition of the house prior to closing.

Buyers should not assume anything.

A lot can happen between you accepting an offer and getting to the closing table. Always keep open the possibility that something could happen prior to closing to delay, or even prevent closing from occurring.

The seller must bring photo identification to the closing. This is required since 9/11.

Be sure to save all your closing paperwork in a safe place!

You will need some of it for your taxes as you may have to report the gain from the sale and pay taxes unless an exclusion applies. If you are eligible for "exclusion of gain from the sale of your personal residence" you won't have to pay taxes on the cash received from the sale if you meet the guidelines for exclusion.

Single $250,000 exclusion possibly available

Married Filing Joint $500,000 exclusion possibly available

To generally qualify you must be in the home 2 of the last five years as an owner occupant.

The satisfaction of deed and other closing documents will be provided to the buyer, and you should file all your closing documents after the sale in either a fireproof box and/or safe deposit box.

The documents are very important and due care should be utilized to safeguard them.

They are an inconvenience to replace and will cost you valuable time and money. Also, **if you are purchasing another property after the sale, be sure to file your homestead exemption** by April 1st of the year after closing in the county or jurisdiction in which the property is located.

In most states you will save on your property taxes (must be owner occupied residence) and it is worth the effort if you are an owner/occupant. You also want to investigate other exemptions that you may qualify for.

At closing, you would transfer the title to the buyer in exchange for the purchase price that is stated in the contract. You would also deliver a deed, title evidence, and a property survey if required. The buyer brings insurance, termite letter, cashier's check etcetera.

You will be required to sign final mortgage papers, IRS Form 1099, and other closing documents. The attorney will explain the purpose of each of these.

In addition, what the seller or buyer brings to closing will vary depending on your locale, so be aware that state laws vary on buyer and seller responsibilities. In addition, who brings what will vary based on how closing costs were negotiated.

In most cases, there are no warranties after closing!

The only defects that a buyer can make notice of or complain about are defects that they can prove were known and/or hidden defects that were not disclosed or could not have been found out about through a reasonable investigation.

Post-Closing is critical. Utilize a cash flow budget. Stay in touch with your agent. Your deed and mortgage proving that you paid off your mortgage will be registered and filed at the county recorder's office if you had not yet paid off the loan prior to selling your home.

On a day when you have time it may be wise to go to the recorder's office a month or more after closing to ensure that the satisfaction of deed and mortgage payoff was properly recorded. In some areas you may be able to verify that the deed and mortgage was properly recorded by doing an online search as many jurisdictions have archived mortgage and tax information for electronic retrieval.

Also remember that all home selling and home buying situations are different and may require a more detailed offer and closing than that listed above. Use the above home selling process as a guide only as each situation will be unique.

Chapter 6 The Steps that You Need to Take If You Plan on Selling Your Home Yourself

For Sale By Owner—what you need to know if you desire to sell your home yourself

If you are attempting to sell your home yourself, you should be aware that those in the real estate industry have a name for those who attempt to sell their home on their own.

Although it is not necessarily meant to be derogatory—those who attempt to sell their home themselves are known as FSBO's (pronounced fizboes) by those in the real estate industry. However, many agents will steer their buyers away from homes that are not listed by real estate agents.

Over the years consumers who have tried to sell their homes themselves have contacted our office after having a difficult time trying to sell their property on their own. In almost all cases the property was overpriced from the start—and/or was not in good selling condition for the current market.

Many did not understand how to price their property right—and in the process did not attract high quality buyers.

This chapter is in large part inspired by those who desire to sell their home themselves—but may lack the "know how" of what needs to be done to sell their home themselves—in a successful manner!

Whether you decide to list with an agent or sell your home yourself, there are certain variables that are common to both. If your home sits on the market for a long time, the less likely it is to sell—or the less you will get for your home.

Your goal should be to sell in a timely manner and at top dollar based on the current market conditions!

You must have a system or approach that you utilize that will lead to you pricing your home right—in the current market.

With residential home inventory being reduced in many parts of the country at this time (Spring 2023)—you want to determine the best price that will bring buyers to your door—right from the start!

If you need starting point to determine what homes are selling for in your area, you can go to the following links:

realtytrac.com

trulia.com

zillow.com

hud.gov

Keep in mind that the above sites are a starting point only—and you will need to do additional pricing research to come up with the true market value for your home!

Many homeowners base their sales price on what they paid for their property, what their property appraised at according to the tax assessor's office, what they owe on their mortgage, or what their neighbor received when they sold their home—which in either of the scenarios above can be off by a substantial amount from the true market value.

You must determine the price that a willing buyer is willing to pay— today as the market is currently configured.

If I fail to purchase, will someone else purchase? That is what should be running through a prospective purchaser's mind—if you price your home right and the home is in good selling condition for the market!

How do I Determine the Right Price?

The right price is derived by determining what others are paying for a similar style house in a similar styled neighborhood, at the current time, or within the last 6 months or so depending on your market and neighborhood. It is important to consider the price of properties actually on the market, those that have recently sold and those that have recently expired (did not sell—normally due to over-pricing) so that you can come up with a price that is competitive and will get you the desired sale in the least amount of time at a fair price to both you and the purchaser!

If you don't have a realtor that can provide you this information— you must use your time and research abilities to discern this information yourself from public sites and agencies in your area.

Keep in mind that you may not get as clear a picture as an agent would get with the data that you gather—however, you would be in better position than other "for sale by owners" who normally don't pursue the pricing of their home in the appropriate manner.

If your home "stands out from the crowd" by being in the best-selling condition based on price and other factors in a buyer's mind—you increase the likelihood of selling your home in a timely manner and at or near your asking price.

Why You Must Price Your Home Right—Right from the Start?

Likewise, if you over-price your home by even a little you could turn away potential buyers by the dozens!

If you price your property right and your property is in the right condition, you should receive several offers within the first 30 days (60 days if you are selling yourself) unless your pricing, selling condition or marketing is out of balance—compared to the market!

It is normally not in your best interest to "test the market" by pricing high and then dropping the price.

It is normally not in your best interest to put your home on the market when your home needs major repairs or upgrades.

Doing so in many cases can lead to buyer turnoff and your home sitting on the market for months with few interested buyers.

And in many cases no qualified or appropriate offers—or you may receive offers that are "below" what the real market value was at the time that you put the property on the market.

Why Home Buyers Must Be Able to "Find" your Property?

When you first decide to sell, and you put your property on the market is when you will normally get the most action. That is the case whether you list your property with a real estate brokerage company—or decide to sell on your own!

The viewing of "new listings" are particularly attractive to home buyers as they have already seen what is on the market and in their price range—if they were utilizing a real estate agent.

If you price too high, you could possibly miss those new buyers during the critical (new period) 14-day period if you were utilizing an agent!

Many agents at real estate companies normally search homes in a certain price range and if you are outside that price range due to overpricing that is one less viewing that could have possibly led to a sale had the property been priced right—right from the start.

By attempting to sell the property yourself many buyers would have no way of knowing that your property was for sale unless they rode by your house or discovered that your home was for sale in some other manner (your marketing mix that you came up with to get the word out that your home is for sale).

OK let's recap—what exactly do you need to do to successfully sell your home yourself:

- Price your home right—right from the start
- Make sure you do the needed repairs prior to putting your home on the market
- A pre-sale inspection can be helpful in many cases
- Consider staging—or reducing the clutter in your home
- Make sure your appliances are clean and up-to-date
- Make sure your HVAC, Plumbing, Water Heater and other systems are in top running condition—replace if necessary
- Always consider the size, condition and improvements of your property—as compared to your competition
- Make sure you know your competition—and price your home accordingly
- Make sure your home is in the best condition based on your sales price

Even if you are trying to sell your home as an owner—if you price it right and your property is in the right selling condition in a desirable area you can be successful. Just be sure that you have the proper mindset and time commitment that is needed.

Selling your home, yourself is not an easy task—however if you approach the process with a "comprehensive understanding" of what it takes, and you are committed to doing what is necessary—you can be successful.

You must be ready to accept an offer, determine the credit worthiness of a buyer, coordinate closing, get the required repairs and other contingencies done in a timely manner—along with all the "unexpected" that can occur from contract to closing!

We wish you success in the sale of your current home as well as success in the purchase of your future home!

91

Chapter 7 The Top 20 Questions to Ask Your Real Estate Agent & Checklist for Success

In this chapter you will be presented with pressing questions that you want to ask your potential or current real estate agent so that you can put yourself and your family in a better position for the selling of your home.

If you are selling your home as a "cash sale" some of the questions may not be relevant, however they are still important to know as you may have a need to use leverage (lending) on a future purchase or sale.

> It is important that you realize that you must ask and receive the right answers to questions that you may have when you are interviewing real estate agents to sell your home. Below you will find a list of questions that you should ask real estate agents that you are considering for the selling of your home.

1) How many homes have you sold in this area in the last 18 months?

2) How long have you been in real estate, and do you work full-time or part-time?

3) How many buyers and sellers are you working with currently? That number will tell you if they have the available time and commitment that is needed to sell your home.

4) Do you have a website that I can visit to learn more about you– and your company?

5) What makes you different from any other agent who wants to sell my home?

6) What is the complete home selling process in your opinion?

7) What are closing costs and who will have to pay them?

8) What documents will I have to sign and how long do you expect my home to be on the market in the current economy?

9) Have you ever been disciplined by a real estate board or real estate commission?

10) How often can I expect to hear from you about the status of my property if I list with you?

11) Will I have to "stage my house" or do repairs and remove clutter or do you anticipate it being sold as is? Depending on your selling price and market conditions staging may be helpful.

12) Is your real estate license active and in good standing? Look for a yes or no answer and then later check it out at your state real estate licensing website.

13) What is your level of professionalism and where and how did you receive your real estate education?

14) How long is the listing agreement and do I have to pay a fee if I cancel early. Most listing agreements are normally 3 or 6 months but they are also totally negotiable in most states. A reputable company will not force you to list with them because they will let their "service" do the talking and they will not charge you a cancellation fee.

If they do it may be a cause for concern–however it may be company policy which they have no control over. If there is a fee–

ask if the fee can be waived if you must cancel due to an unforeseen event.

15) What is your plan as far as marketing and selling my house? The use of the MLS service (Multiple Listing Service) is by far (in my opinion) the most effective means of marketing your property (along with the property being in top selling condition and priced right for the market) however a combination of on–and off line advertising will usually provide the best results.

Yard signs, open houses, photos, online marketing and other technologically savvy marketing is a sign that the agent is serious in the selling of your home. What will the agent that you are interviewing do that other agents won't–or can't do?

16) How will we come up with the appropriate price to sell my home? Most agents will provide you "comparable properties" that have recently sold in your area that is like your home (often called CMA's or comps). The more similar the "comps" and the closer in proximity to your home–the better the "comps" are.

17) What are the fees that I will have to pay you to list and sell my house? In most states fees are negotiable. However, there are many variations of the fee structure.   Most brokers normally have an acceptable range in which they are willing to go–while others offer a flat fee type of arrangement or a variation. In most states– fees are almost always negotiable.

18) Will the agent handle the paperwork–or will it be delegated to other agents or team members.   Will the listing agent handle negotiations, verify that buyers are qualified, coordinate closing and ensure that all actions are performed in a timely manner?

19) Have the Broker or Your Company been involved in any disputes with buyers/sellers in the last 5 years–and if so–how were they resolved. Depending on the market and the activity of agents in a particular office–that may not necessarily be a bad thing. However, it is good to know if they have had disputes between buyers and sellers and to know if they were satisfactorily resolved.

20) What do you feel is important based on all that you know about my property and my future goals?

After the sale of your home, you may purchase another property that will need to be financed and you want to ask your potential real estate professional the following questions:

1. **How do you go about pre-qualifying your client for a mortgage loan?**

2. **How will I know that the mortgage loan type you recommend is best for me (us)?**

3. **Why do I have to put an Earnest Money Deposit on the property and what exactly is the purpose of the deposit?**

4. **What does closing costs consist of and who should pay them and why?**

5. Who gets to choose the closing attorney and who will they represent?

6. Why are real estate taxes community association assessments, utilities, and other fees pro-rated?

7. Can I (we) unilaterally extend the closing date and for how long?

8. Can you explain the types of deeds available and what type will I get assuming I purchase the property in question?

9. Is a survey, termite letter and title insurance required and who will pay for it?

10.   If the property is damaged prior to closing what is my (our) recourse?

11.   Whose responsibility is it to inspect the property and neighborhood?

12. What is the due diligence period, and should I choose to purchase this property as-is or subject to a due diligence period?

13. If the deal falls through, who keeps the earnest money that I (we) submitted with the contract?

14. What are agency relationships, and which one do you recommend, and why?

15. Who pays the brokerage commission?

16. What's the seller's/buyer's disclosure requirements and how will it benefit me (us)?

17. As a real estate agent what are your legal requirements for disclosure?

18. How must notice of acceptance be delivered and in what form?

19. What are other provisions that you feel are important?

20. What are exhibits, addenda, and special stipulations and why are they needed?

If they are hesitant and/or can't adequately answer and explain or clarify in a manner that you can understand, you might want to select another real estate agent.

The Most Important 10 Questions that You Need to Ask Yourself

Home Seller Checklist for Success

1) Am I properly prepared to sell at this time?

Y or N

2) Have I completed my personal financial statements (especially my cash flow statement at a minimum) and are they satisfactory?

Y or N

3) Ask your agent if the buyer has applied for loan and received a firm loan commitment according to the timelines in the contract. Have I maximized my credit score to the best of my ability based on my current financial position? Have I made myself aware of the need to obtain a termite/pest letter, survey and any other concerns?

Y or N

4) Do I know the type of loan that the buyer will select and is there a high likelihood that the loan will be approved and closing will occur? (have I sold with the end in mind)?

Y or N

5) Will I pay closing costs (OR WILL WE SPLIT THE COSTS) and select the closing attorney or will the buyer, do it?

Y or N

6) Have I checked out the environmental concerns that I have inside the house, neighborhood, and surrounding community?

Are the results of the home inspection (that I or home buyer did) satisfactory or are repairs needed before we can close on this property?

Y or N

7) Do I know how to apply for the homestead exemption and other exemptions that I may be entitled to, along with securing all my closing and other important paperwork after I close on my next home if I plan on purchasing a move-up home?

Y or N

8) Do I know how to check and see if my mortgage and warranty deed payoff has been properly recorded after the sale and if my mortgage and warranty deed has been properly recorded after my next home purchase (if applicable)?

Y or N

9) Do I know if my GFE **(now called Loan Estimate),** HUD-1 **(now called Closing Disclosure)** are accurate (what I expected) and have I previewed it prior to closing?

Y or N

10) Have I done a final walk through and am I comfortable with the upcoming closing date and all the terms of the contract, including repairs that were required based on the inspection and negotiation—and do I have a plan to remove all of my belongings by the closing date?

Y or N

By utilizing this helpful guide appropriately, you will easily put yourself ahead of most home sellers when it comes to selling your home. Enjoy the success that you are about to achieve and enjoy your successful selling period that is in store for you.

BONUS SECTION (FAQ's that can broaden your home selling and home buying awareness)

Q: Why do I need a down payment to purchase a home?

A: Even though you may qualify for a 100% loan if your credit score is high enough or you may receive down payment assistance it is important from a psychological point of view to not only put money down but to have an established emergency fund.

By doing the above I have found that homeowners find ownership more rewarding, and they tend to be able to weather financial storms that come their way.

With little or no down payment I have seen purchasers walk away from their obligations due to frustration and hopelessness. The key is to do all you can on the front end to prevent getting into a situation where you will be forced to walk away or find yourself in a hopeless situation.

Q: What are the down payment assistance programs available?

A: There are many programs available at the local and state level. There are also targeted homebuyer incentives for police/firefighters, educators, and nurses available in many areas of the country. HUD also offer low down payment options on some of its inventory of homes.

Q: How can I improve my credit situation and credit scores before I purchase my house?

A: It all begins by properly analyzing where you are at credit wise. That means pulling your credit reports and obtaining your credit scores. From that point you will know what you need to do to bring your score up and clean up your credit reports if there is a need to do so.

Q: What Is the Complete Home Buying Process in Your Opinion?

A: It starts with preliminary homebuyer prequalification to post-closing in my opinion and based on the way our company operates.

A professional real estate agent should be concerned with more than just your ability to purchase a home, they should also be concerned with your ability to maintain and keep your new home.

Therefore, "preliminary pre-qualification" is a vital step. Don't skip this step, many homeowners have skipped this step in the past to their own peril (loss of house, financial difficulty etcetera)

The home buying process begins well before you decide to place an offer on a home.

The preparation that you put into buying a home on the front end will pay great dividends on the back end if you do it the proper way.

I often have the home buyer or home seller pull their credit reports and obtain their credit scores.

Although they may not see it now this will help them start to take control of their financial affairs if they aren't doing so already. Assuming their credit and credit scores are satisfactory we move on to the next step.

A quick front end and back-end ratio analysis is then performed.

If their credit and credit score situation is unsatisfactory, they correct them (usually within 12 months) and we then move to the next step.

Assuming you have no bankruptcies, judgments, or other public record data on your report it can normally be cleaned up within 12 months if you have the right cash flow and are disciplined in paying off outstanding debt and paying your revolving and installment accounts in a timely manner.

I often have the potential home buyer pull their credit from the three major credit bureaus and have them obtain their credit scores as well. This gives the consumer confidence that they are in control of their own financial destiny.

While working with buyer's I try to implement a comprehensive strategy in their home buying pursuit.

It is important to begin at the cash flow (budget) analysis point and move forward from there. I look at their total financial situation so I can be of the most benefit to them (assuming they agree to the complimentary service).

From there we can see if there is discretionary income available after all variable and fixed expenses have been paid.

I then perform personal balance sheet, income statement and net worth analysis to get an even better look at their financial situation so I can be of the most benefit to them (again assuming they agree to the complimentary service).

Front and back-end ratio analysis would then be performed again.

I then analyze all of this based on family size, future goals (retirement, college, etc.) financial needs and wants and other factors that may be present in their situation.

I then decide if they qualify based on their down payment saved, emergency fund, cash flow situation and their ability to reach their goals based on what they stated above.

I also look at other factors (compensating) and non-compensating as well--such as a future financial windfall, other household income that will not be included on the loan application, expected increase in family size, child going to college and any other factor that could potentially have a negative or positive effect on their home purchase.

Assuming all the above turns out to be positive I inform them of the home buying process in greater detail.

I then inform them of the advantages of getting pre-approved as opposed to pre-qualified (more negotiating power).

Be aware that not all real estate agents will be concerned with your "preliminary pre-qualification" but you should be--you have to live with the choice and decision you make well into the future, so it is important that you get this step right.

Once they are pre-approved, we begin the home search and once a home is found to their liking we put an offer contract on that property (along with earnest money deposit).

After negotiation and a final sales price and terms are agreed to the buyer performs an inspection (usually a professional inspector is hired) based on the time limits specified in the offer.

If there are problems of concern to the purchaser, we counter the offer and negotiate until a final sales price is agreed to. Once all contingencies are met the contract moves forward and the closing occurs.

Once the contract is accepted you make formal application for the loan (unless buying with cash) and once you receive the loan commitment letter (a contract between you and the lender---make sure you understand what you are signing) and the process moves forward.

Once the inspection is complete and repairs are negotiated the contract continues to move forward. If no agreement is reached the contract may become null and void.

Assuming the contract moves forward and closing approaches after you receive your mortgage commitment, the attorney will submit a title insurance binder along with other legal paperwork required by your lender.

Once everybody has signed off approval a closing date can be set.

It is highly recommended that you do a final walk through of your soon to be new home prior to closing.

The final walk through allows you to reconfirm the condition of the house prior to closing. This normally happens a day or two before closing.

Don't skip this step because this is usually your last chance to verify that there has been no change or damage to the property, all agreed on repairs have been made, appliances you expect to be there are still there and that the seller's personal belongings have been removed.

Don't assume anything. A lot can happen between having your offer accepted and getting to the closing table.

If possible, it is not a bad idea to do another walk through several hours before closing just as an added security and peace of mind effort.

Make sure that you bring photo identification to the closing. This is required since 9/11.

Real estate closing can often be exciting and stressful at the same time.

There are many legal papers being shuffled back and forth, as well as checks for large sums of money being exchanged among parties.

One form of paperwork you want to get right is the **"proper titling of your home"** as that is critical for your and your family's future success.

You want to know how you want your property titled prior to closing so be sure to run that by your agent, attorney, and possibly other professionals.

At closing, the seller gives the title to the buyer in exchange for the purchase price that is stated in the contract. The seller also delivers a deed, title evidence, property survey if required. The buyer brings insurance, termite letter, cashier's check etc.

You will be required to sign final mortgage papers, IRS Form 1099, a form known as the HUD-1 statement **(now called the Closing Disclosure)** or Uniform Settlement Statement and other closing documents.

The attorney will explain the purpose of each of these at the closing.

In addition, what the seller or buyer brings to closing will vary depending on your locale, so be aware that state laws vary on buyer and seller responsibilities.

In addition, who brings what will vary based on how closing costs were negotiated by you and your agent!

In most cases, there are no warranties after closing.

The only defects that you can make notice of or complain about are defects that you can prove were known and/or hidden defects that were not disclosed or could not have been found out about through a reasonable investigation.

Post-Closing is critical. Continue to utilize a cash flow or budget throughout your period of homeownership and you can really get ahead financially. Also, stay in touch with your real estate agent.

Your deed and mortgage will be registered and filed at the county recorder's office.

On a day when you have time it may be wise to go to the recorder's office a month or more after closing to ensure that the deed and mortgage was properly recorded.

Be sure to save all your closing paperwork in a safe place. You will need some of it for your taxes as interest, points, and now MIP or PMI is now deductible on your tax return.

The deed and abstract should be placed in either a fireproof box and/or safe deposit box.

The documents are very important and due care should be utilized to safeguard them. They are an inconvenience to replace and will cost you valuable time and money.

Also file your **"homestead exemption"** by April 1st (or other designated deadline in your area) of the year after closing in the County in which the property is purchased.

In many states you will save on your property taxes (must be owner occupied residence) and it is worth the effort if you are an owner/occupant.

The above home buying process assumes 1st time buyer with no house to sell!

Also remember that all home buying situations are different and may require a more detailed offer and closing than that listed above.

Use the above home buying process as a guide only as each situation will be unique.

Q: You comment quite a bit on your site about "selling a home the right or smart way. What makes you so sure that the way you suggest is the "right way"? Isn't that a subjective opinion?

A: Yes, in a sense you could say that it is subjective, however it is also based on over 15 years of real world (objective) behavior of many of my past clients.

The preliminary home preparation process is a proven success. In addition, intuitively it makes financial sense to analyze your cash flow, pay down your debts to a manageable level, create an adequate emergency fund, keep your house payment at a reasonable ratio so you are not "house poor", and other positive financial moves prior to making what many consider the biggest sale of their life.

Be advised that no system or approach to home selling is 100%, however doing the above will greatly increase the odds of your home sale being an enjoyable endeavor and you will be thankful you did it the right way well into the future.

Furthermore, when you contrast the normal home selling process with that of the "smart way to sell" there can be no dispute that "the right or smart way to sell your home" is far superior.

Q: As a Home Seller should I get a Home Warranty on the next home that I purchase?

A: The choice of whether you should get a home warranty can often be a difficult one. It is imperative that you have the home properly inspected, you know the age of the home along with the age and working condition of the appliances, plumbing and HVAC systems.

Home warranties generally cover appliances, heating and air conditioning and plumbing.

Whether or not a Home Warranty policy is appropriate for you will depend on your personal situation, from finances to your risk tolerance level.

Q: I bought a time share several years ago and I now want to sell. Are there any good companies out there that can sell it for me?

A: Although I rarely deal with timeshares this is what I have seen in this industry for the most part.

Most companies that I have seen as of late are charging a listing fee and in most cases, they don't sell the time share. In cases when they do it is usually at a steep discount.

I have not come across a really good company out there to sell your time share through.

That is not to say there is not one out there, but I have not come across one in recent years.

It is my opinion you never should have bought a time share as it was initially a bad purchase unless you totally loved the area and planned on using it religiously.

You should have purchased the time share at the beginning with the end in mind. At that point you would have realized that trying to sell a time share without incurring a loss was highly improbable.

However, savvy time share sales agents only tell you about the pleasant side of owning a timeshare for the most part.

Time shares that were purchased for 15 thousand dollars or more are now selling for less than 2 thousand dollars in many parts of the country.

It may be best to try to sell to someone who is at the timeshare during the week you have bought out for the time share instead of using a potential rip-off company.

You can also utilize the various media (print, web, word of mouth, flyers etcetera) to get the word out that you have a time share for sale. Just be aware that they are practically worthless in most cases and expect a low offer if you get any offers at all.

Q: Should I Purchase My Atlanta Area Home as A Lease Purchase?

A: Many Lease-Purchase homes are often advertised by sellers in local newspapers, on for sale signs, the internet and other media and potential homebuyers often seek them out in their strong desire to own their own home.

Let's look at the potential lease-purchase from a buyer's and seller's perspective.

As a purchaser if you did not initiate the lease-purchase offer or someone who represents (i.e., agent, attorney etcetera) you did not initiate it, the offer will more than likely not be in your best interest.

This is usually what occurs when a potential home buyer sees a lease-purchase ad in the various media and respond to it. They usually have no idea of the home buying or financial planning process and want to own a home at all costs.

They will be easy prey for a savvy home seller and/or their representative because they are not fully aware of the process, and they are not in proper position to negotiate the terms and price.

Sellers and/or their representatives normally will structure the sales contract in a manner that will maximize the terms and sales price to their benefit and minimize the terms and sales price to your (purchaser's) benefit.

Those are some of the reasons I dislike lease-purchases from the buyer's perspective.

In addition, at the end of the lease purchase you will be locked into that specific property at the specific price that you agreed to, regardless of market conditions.

If prices of homes have risen or fallen, you are locked in. The purpose of a lease purchase is normally to buy the purchaser time so that they can get their credit to a level where they can qualify for a loan at a good rate.

Once you qualify for a loan at a good rate you have the potential to purchase ANY property, so why limit yourself to one particular house.

Most lease purchases offered through Multiple Listing Services where you deal with real estate agents are usually for one year and usually not more than two, as real estate agents are concerned about their commission and will normally not accept an offer beyond that period.

Other sellers who offer lease purchases without the assistance of an agent may offer a longer lease-term than three years, but they will more than compensate for the longer term by structuring the terms and sales price in their favor.

If you must purchase a lease-purchase it is imperative that you draft the terms and sales price yourself or with the assistance of a competent real estate agent or other professional.

A better option if you feel you really want the property and don't want to lose out may be a lease "option" purchase where you are not locked into that purchase, and you can opt in or opt out.

Again, structuring the terms and purchase price is key so make sure you utilize competent professionals.

An even better option (and one that I really like) for you may be to continue renting and get your credit score and reports to a level where you qualify for an FHA or Conventional loan at prevailing market rates (competitive interest rate) and then purchase the home of your choice with no lease purchase premium included or a lease option fee included.

Again, make sure you have a low debt load, you are pre-approved as opposed to pre-qualified, you have a six-month emergency fund or other compensating factors at work, and you are properly positioned to purchase.

By being ready, willing, and able to purchase you and your agent should be able to negotiate a better deal in most cases than if you were to go the lease-purchase or lease option route.

Q: We are hearing about tough times in the housing industry. With the $8,000 home buyer credit in place is now the right time to buy a home.

A: Only if you are properly prepared to purchase. If you are a first-time buyer with good credit and money saved for a down payment and have a well-established emergency fund or have other compensating factors now is a fantastic time to buy.

On the other hand, if you have questionable credit, unstable job prospects, insufficient down payment, insufficient emergency fund and outstanding debt at an unacceptable level now may not be the best time for you to purchase a home regardless of the credits or incentives that are being offered now, or at a future date.

Q: After the selling of my home, will preparing my taxes be difficult?

A: If you have prepared your own taxes in the past, you may feel comfortable continuing to do your own taxes.

However, there are some nuances that are unique to home selling that you must be aware of. However, if you get up to speed on the current home ownership issues and filing requirements after a home sale that is in the current tax code, you may put yourself in position to continue preparing your own taxes.

For income tax preparation you can utilize the tax professional of your choice—or if your tax situation is not very complicated after your home sale you can choose among the following:

www.HRBlock.com

www.turbotax.intuit.com

www.onepricetaxes.com

If you live in many large metro areas in the United States, you can possibly get free tax preparation if you meet income eligibility and family size guidelines through the United Way VITA program.

116

WEBSITES—If you have further questions or concerns about the content in this book I can be contacted through the following websites:

TheWealthIncreaser.com

www.the-best-atlanta-real-estate-advice.com

www.realty-1-strategic-advisors.com

Thanks for your purchase and may untold success be in your future...

Thomas (TJ) Underwood

ISBN 978-1-953994-06-6

Thomas (TJ) Underwood is the Real Estate Broker at Realty 1 Strategic Advisors, LLC one of the most successful real estate and financial planning companies in the metropolitan Atlanta area. Realty 1 Strategic Advisors is based in Peachtree City, GA.

He is a former fee-only financial planner and top producing loan processor, and he has assisted clients from as far away as Germany with their home sale and financial concerns.

The concepts in **Home Seller 411 *The Smart Guide to Selling Your Home*** have been utilized by savvy home sellers to enhance their home selling efforts.

www.ingramcontent.com/pod-product-compliance
Lightning Source LLC
Chambersburg PA
CBHW061148040426
42445CB00013B/1618